U0483712

符号中国 SIGNS OF CHINA

梅兰竹菊

PLUM BLOSSOM, ORCHID, BAMBOO AND CHRYSANTHEMUM

"符号中国"编写组 ◎ 编著

中央民族大学出版社
China Minzu University Press

图书在版编目(CIP)数据

梅兰竹菊：汉文、英文 / "符号中国"编写组编著. —北京：中央民族大学出版社, 2024.3
（符号中国）
ISBN 978-7-5660-2297-4

Ⅰ. ①梅…　Ⅱ. ①符…　Ⅲ. ①中华文化－介绍－汉、英　Ⅳ. ①K203

中国国家版本馆CIP数据核字（2024）第017487号

符号中国：梅兰竹菊　PLUM BLOSSOM, ORCHID, BAMBOO AND CHRYSANTHEMUM

编　　著	"符号中国"编写组
策划编辑	沙　平
责任编辑	满福玺
英文指导	李瑞清
英文编辑	邱　械
美术编辑	曹　娜　郑亚超　洪　涛
出版发行	中央民族大学出版社
	北京市海淀区中关村南大街27号　邮编：100081
	电话：（010）68472815（发行部）　传真：（010）68933757（发行部）
	（010）68932218（总编室）　　　　（010）68932447（办公室）
经 销 者	全国各地新华书店
印 刷 厂	北京兴星伟业印刷有限公司
开　　本	787 mm×1092 mm　1/16　印张：9.5
字　　数	130千字
版　　次	2024年3月第1版　2024年3月第1次印刷
书　　号	ISBN 978-7-5660-2297-4
定　　价	58.00元

版权所有　侵权必究

"符号中国"丛书编委会

唐兰东　巴哈提　杨国华　孟靖朝　赵秀琴

本册编写者

王　静

前言 Preface

从古至今，梅、兰、竹、菊始终是深受中国人喜爱的四种植物。人们不仅种植它们，还用诗文书画来赞美它们。

梅、兰、竹、菊都是中国土生土长的植物，都具有极强的观赏性。冬日可赏傲雪凌寒的梅花，春天可赏幽香沁人的兰花，秋季可赏傲霜绽放的菊花，而四时常青的则是翠竹。在中国的儒家文化中，"君子"为有道德品格的人，需要恪守节操，坚持自我不断完善，还要以自身的行为来宣示道

Since ancient times, plum blossom, orchid, bamboo and chrysanthemum have been deeply loved by the Chinese who not only plant them but employ poetry, calligraphy and painting to sing their praises.

Plum blossom, orchid, bamboo and chrysanthemum are all native to China and of high ornamental value. You can appreciate the plum blossom that defies the wintry snow, relish the intoxicating smell of the orchid flower in spring, gaze in awe at the chrysanthemum that blooms loftily against the bitter frost in the autumn sunshine, or simply abandon yourself to the evergreen bamboos. According to Chinese Confucian culture, a gentleman always distinguishes with moral integrity, seeks continuous self-improvement, shows his nobility by righteous behaviors, and thus becomes a shining model of decorum that the world will follow. Since the natural properties of plum blossom, orchid, bamboo and chrysanthemum exactly fit all the requirements of a gentleman, they are collectively referred to as the Four Gentlemen in Chinese culture.

A good knowledge of plum blossom, orchid, bamboo and chrysanthemum will further help to grasp the very rich meaning of the Four Gentlemen in the eyes of Chinese, and simultaneously grant you a glimpse of the spiritual core of the traditional Chinese culture.

德的高尚，以此成为世人效法的楷模。梅、兰、竹、菊的自然属性正契合了中国文化中的君子文化，因而被称为"四君子"。

认识了中国的梅、兰、竹、菊，进而就会理解中国人眼中"四君子"所蕴含的丰富含义，也会了解中国传统文化的一部分精神内核。

目录 Contents

说梅
Ode to the Plum Blossom 001

梅之品赏
Appreciation of Plum Blossom 002

梅之精神
Spirit of Plum Blossom 023

墨梅暗香
Delicate Fragrance of Ink Plum Blossom 032

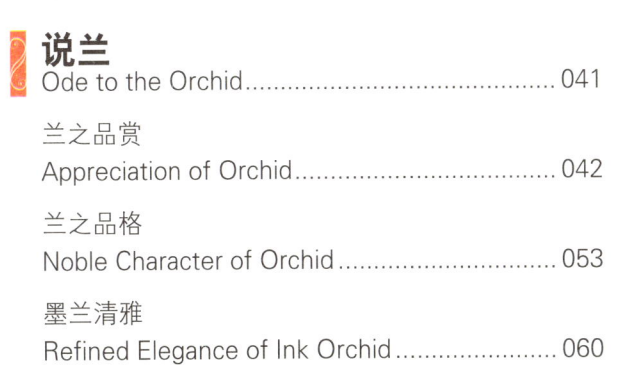

说兰
Ode to the Orchid 041

兰之品赏
Appreciation of Orchid 042

兰之品格
Noble Character of Orchid 053

墨兰清雅
Refined Elegance of Ink Orchid 060

说竹
Ode to the Bamboo 069

竹之品赏
Appreciation of Bamboo 070

竹之风骨
Strong Character of Bamboo 080

竹之生活
Bamboo's Life 089

墨竹潇洒
Natural Charm of Ink Bamboo 108

说菊
Ode to the Chrysanthemum 113

菊之品赏
Appreciation of Chrysanthemum 114

菊之心境
Temper of Chrysanthemum 127

墨菊五色
Five Colors of Ink Chrysanthemum 135

说梅
Ode to the Plum Blossom

　　梅是蔷薇科的落叶小乔木，别名又叫"春梅""干枝梅"，具有喜阳不耐积水的特性。梅是一种先开花后长叶的植物，花朵单生或双朵齐出，有五瓣，花色有白、红、淡绿、淡红等，以白色和淡红色为主，清香幽远。核果球形，未熟时为青色，成熟后呈黄色，味道极酸。梅树一般可生长数十年，有的甚至可达千年以上。

Plum, also known as spring plum or dry plum, is a small deciduous tree of the Rosaceae family. It is a plant typical of sunny habitats but intolerant of excess water. Plum usually blossom first and then comes into leaf. Its flowers can be single or in pairs, yet all have five petals, red, light green and mostly white or pale red in color, with a gentle fragrance. The drupe is round in shape, usually assumes green before maturity and then ripens into yellow and tastes quite acid. In general a plum can grow as long as decades, and for those of unusual longevity even a thousand years cannot deprive their vigor of life.

> 梅之品赏

中国是梅的故乡，已有3000多年的栽培和应用历史。而首先得到先民们重视的不是梅的花朵，而是它的果实——梅子。梅子最早是被当作日常饮食的必需品来看待的，与盐同等重要，其作用大致相当于今天的醋。中国现存最早的史书《尚书》有云："若作和羹，尔唯盐梅。"意思是制作美味羹汤，就要用盐和梅子，贤臣的重要性，就好比做羹汤时用的盐和梅子那样。可见梅子在当时人们生活中起着十分重要的作用。

成书于春秋时期的诗歌总集《诗经》中有一首著名的情诗《摽有梅》，讲的是在暮春时节，梅子黄熟，纷纷坠落。一位姑娘见此

> Appreciation of Plum Blossom

Native to China, plum has been planted and used for more than three thousand years. However, at the beginning the ancestors did not pay much attention to the plum blossom. Instead, it was the fruit that they relished, which was originally regarded as one of the necessities of the daily diet no less important than salt, and in role roughly equivalent to today's vinegar. As the *Classic of History*, the earliest extant Chinese book of its kind, records, "For a hearty soup, salt and plum are quite essential." In fact, it means that salt and plum are essential to make a delicious soup, and a wise minister is as important as the salt and plum used to make the soup. Hence we can see the crucial role that plum played in people's life at that time.

● 枝头的青梅
Greengages on the Branch

情景，联想到时光无情，自己青春流逝，却婚嫁无期，不禁以梅子起兴，唱出了对爱情的渴求。这首诗说明，当时人们种植梅树已十分普遍。在湖南长沙的马王堆汉墓的出土文物中，有一些陶罐里面放有完好的梅核和梅干，这说明在西汉初期，长江流域的人早已引种、栽培梅树，并利用梅子加工食品了。在栽种梅树、采摘加工梅子的同时，人们逐渐喜爱并欣赏梅花的色彩和姿态之美。而且在长期的栽培过程中，个别植株出现了复瓣、重瓣，

There is a famous love lyric called *Ripe Plums Are Falling* complied in the *Book of Songs*, a collection of poems composed during the Spring and Autumn Period (770 B.C.-476 B.C.). It tells a story in late spring when a girl sees the plums ripen and fall, she cannot but think of the ruthless time that hastens the passage of youth whereas she herself remains unmarried. Thus by an explicit comparison with the falling plums, she sings the longing for love. Besides, this poem also shows plum trees were very common at that time. From tombs of the Western Han Dynasty at Mawangdui in

● 盛开的梅花
Plum Blossom in Full Bloom

奇异的花瓣或萼片，新奇的枝姿等，于是有人开始着意培育专供观赏的梅花新品种。从西汉时起，"花梅"开始逐渐从"果梅"中分出来，成为独立的一大品类。

今天，梅树经过长期的人工培植，已是拥有数百个品种的大家族，主要分"果梅"和"花梅"两大系统。果梅可分为青梅、白梅、红梅等，用于食用；而花梅则以观赏为主，生长姿态各不相同。按照梅枝的姿态不同，花梅又可分为直枝类、垂枝类和龙游类三种。直枝梅是中国梅花中最常见、品种最

Changsha City, Hunan Province, there have excavated some pots with intact plum stones and prunes in it, which indicates that in the early Western Han Dynasty, people along the Yangtze River had already begun to introduce and cultivate plum, and also use the fruit to process food. It might be at the same time that people gradually found delight in it and started to appreciate the color and elegant posture of the plum blossom. Moreover, in the long-term course of cultivation, some individual plum may turn out with double petals, strange sepals or novel postures, so people began to cultivate new varieties of ornamental plums deliberately. Since the Western Han Dynasty, the flowering plum cultivars had been separated from the fruiting ones and gradually developed into a large independent category.

After a long period of cultivation, now plum has become a large family with hundreds of cultivars. It can mainly divide into fruiting plum and flowering plum. The former may yield edible fruit, such as greengage, white plum, red plum and so on, whereas the latter is raised as ornamentals. And as its branches may assume gestures of all kinds, the flowering plum can further

寿阳公主的梅花妆

南北朝时期,赏梅、咏梅之风日盛。据史籍记载,南朝宋武帝的女儿寿阳公主有一日躺卧在皇宫含章殿的檐下小憩,恰好有一阵微风吹来,园中的梅花纷纷落下,其中有几朵碰巧落到了寿阳公主的额头上,在她前额上留下了梅花样的淡淡花痕,拂拭不去,使寿阳公主显得更加娇柔妩媚。皇后见了,十分喜欢。此后,爱美的寿阳公主便时常摘几片梅花贴在自己前额上。宫女们见了,个个称奇,并跟着仿效起来。不久,这种被人们称为"梅花妆"的妆饰方式便在宫中流传开来,并很快流传到民间,受到了女孩子们的喜爱。唐代诗人牛峤有"若缀寿阳公主额,六宫争肯学梅妆"的诗句,说的就是这个典故。

Plum Blossom Makeup of Princess Shouyang

During the Southern and Northern dynasties (420-589), the fashion prevailed to appreciate and laud the plum blossom in poetic forms. According to historical records, one day Princess Shouyang, daughter of Emperor Wu of the Song of the Southern dynasties in the Southern dynasties, was resting under the eaves of Hanzhang Palace in the imperial garden. Then a sudden breeze rustled the plum trees, and among all the fallen plum blossom, several by chance drifted down onto her fair face, leaving a faint yet indelible floral imprint on her forehead that enhanced her beauty further. Since the queen was also very fond of it, from then on the young princess who loved beauty so much often picked a few plum blossom to paste on her forehead. The court ladies were said to be so impressed, that they started decorating their own foreheads likewise. Very soon this cosmetic design known as plum blossom makeup became popular in the palace, then widespread among the folk and won great favor among girls. Niu Qiao, a Chinese poet in the Tang Dynasty once alluded to this story in a poem, "As the plum blossom happened to decorate Princess Shouyang's forehead and add to her charm, all court ladies strived to learn this plum blossom makeup."

- 明刻本《历代百美图》——寿阳公主
Princess Shouyang in the Block-printed *Beauties in All Ages*, Ming Dynasty (1368-1644)

● 枝条扭曲的龙游梅（图片提供：FOTOE）
Tortuous Plum with Twisted Branches

多、变化最广的一类；垂枝梅的枝条自然下垂或斜出，形成独立的伞状树态；而龙游梅的枝条扭曲，姿态奇特，富有韵味。

梅树喜欢在温暖而稍湿润的气候中生长，所以在长江流域及西南地区栽培极广。人们传统上认为梅花能在冬天傲雪开放，其实它也是有极限温度的，开花至少也需要平均气温达到6℃—7℃。

由于梅花忍耐严寒、傲雪早

divide into upright plum, pendulous plum and tortuous plum. The upright plum is most commonly seen, most numerous in variety, and also allows a maximum of gestures. The pendulous plum, however, has the branches droop naturally and thus postures like an unfurled umbrella. The tortuous plum grows just as its name suggests, the twisted branches result in peculiar poses yet simultaneously retain a lingering charm.

Plum trees grow best in a warm and slightly humid climate, so people usually

垂枝梅花
Pendulous plum blossom

发，具有一种不屈不挠的斗争精神，中国古代文人爱梅、咏梅、画梅，爱梅花的风姿，更希望能够成为像梅花一样高洁的人。久而久之，赏梅还形成了具体的审美标准，主要是观梅花之色、品梅花之香、赏梅花之姿。

梅花花色包括紫红、粉红、淡黄、淡墨、纯白等多种，以白色和淡红色最为常见。纯白色的梅花清雅香寒，而盛开在雪中的红梅则热烈奔放，蕴含着无限生机，为寒冷

cultivate them around the Yangtze River and in the southwest of China. Although tradition has it that the plum can blossom defying cold and snow, still the plant has its own temperature range. Generally its flowering needs an average temperature up to at least 6°C-7°C (42.8F-44.6F).

Since the plum blossom is more tolerant of bitter cold than other flowers and often blooms earlier against the wintry snow, it symbolizes an indomitable fighting spirit. The ancient Chinese literati indeed treasured it to

● 直枝梅花中的玉蝶梅
Upright Jade Butterfly Plum Blossom

煮酒论英雄

"煮酒论英雄"的故事出自古典长篇小说《三国演义》第二十一回。一天,曹操派人请刘备一起饮酒,二人以青梅下酒,谈论起"当今天下谁可称为英雄"的话题。刘备先后提出几位当时势力较大的地方军阀,曹操认为他们都虚有其表,不是真正的英雄。最后,曹操说:"今天下英雄,惟使君与操耳!"(现在天下的英雄,只有你和我了!)刘备一听,吃了一惊,手中的筷子也不觉掉在地下。正巧这时突然天降大雨,雷声大作,刘备急忙低下身拾起筷子,并说是因为被雷声吓到才掉了筷子,巧妙地掩饰了内心的惊惶。通过这次酒局,曹操的傲视群雄之态、雄霸天下之志表露无遗。而刘备能够随机应变、进退自如,也表现出了一世豪杰所应有的机智与城府。

Cao Cao and Liu Bei Judging the Heroes of the Age over Hot Plum Wine

This story is taken from Chapter 21 in the classical novel *Romance of the Three Kingdoms*. One day, Cao Cao invited Liu Bei for a drinking. Over the plum and wine, they began to talk about the heroes of the age. Liu Bei proposed several local warlords of enormous influence at their times, but Cao Cao thought that they were only impressive in appearance and hence not real heroes. Finally Cao Cao pointed out, "The only heroes in the world are you and I." Liu Bei was stunned at the words, his chopsticks rattling to the floor. And just at that moment the storm burst with a tremendous peal of thunder and rush of rain, so he quickly stooped down to pick up the chopsticks, excusing that they were dropped because of the shock of thunder, and thus skillfully covering up his inner panic. This meeting fully exposed Cao Cao's self-esteem over all rivals and his ambition to dominate the world. Liu Bei's witty response to circumstances also revealed the utmost tact and shrewdness of a real hero.

- 曹操像
Portrait of Cao Cao

粉红色的梅花
Pink Plum Blossom

雪中红梅（图片提供：FOTOE）
Red Plum Blossom in the Snow

的冬季增添了暖暖春意。各色梅花之中，又以绿梅最为名贵。绿梅又称"绿萼梅"，花瓣纯白，而花蒂和花萼却是绿色，花梗也为青色，洁白的花瓣在绿色萼托、枝条的映衬下略微发绿，更显淡雅高贵，所以自古以来被人们推为梅中秀品。

赏梅，离不开品梅之香。梅花的香气是中国古代文人极为推崇的。宋代诗人卢梅坡的《雪梅》写道：

梅雪争春未肯降，
骚人搁笔费评章。
梅须逊雪三分白，
雪却输梅一段香。

此诗的大意是：梅花和雪花都认为各自占尽了春色，谁也不肯服输。这可难坏了诗人，难以写出评判谁更佳的文章。说句公道话，梅花不如雪花晶莹洁白，而雪花却没有梅花那一股清香。为了衬托出梅花所独具的清香，人们通常还会把桃花、杏花等与梅花做对比，桃花虽然美艳动人，但是在文人看来，桃花的芬芳多少有些甜腻，与梅花的"清香""暗香"是无法相提并论的。南宋

a great extent, they sang highly of the plum blossom in poems, or painted its graceful bearing, hoping that they could become as virtuous as the flower itself. Thus over a long period of time, specific aesthetic standards have been set for plum appreciation, mainly including observation of its color, relish of its fragrance, and appraisal of its posture.

The plum blossom can be varied in color. Most of them are white or pale red, but we may also see purple, pink, light yellow or pale black ones. The pure white plum blossom usually has elegant and cold fragrance, whereas the red one that blooms in snow rather resembles an outburst of enthusiasm with boundless vigor which lends the cold winter a warm touch of spring. Among all, the green plum blossom is most valuable and rare. Also known as green-sepaled plum blossom, it has pure white petals yet green pedicel, calyx, and footstalk. Thus set off by the green background, the white petals are slightly tinged with green and appear more elegant and of higher nobility. Therefore since ancient times the green plum blossom has been crowned as queen of its kind.

The appreciation of plum blossom cannot do without the relish of its

• 淡雅的绿梅
Elegant Green Plum Blossom

诗人陆游有诗云："平生不喜凡桃李，看了梅花睡过春。"而另一位诗人吕本中也曾写道："不将供俗鼻，愈更觉清香。"意思就是说，梅花之香是专供雅人品赏的，非一般俗人所能理解。中国古代以"梅香"取名的女子极多，究其原委，或许正是出于对梅花香气的喜爱吧。

古代文人赏梅的标准，归纳起来有"四贵"，即"贵稀不贵繁，贵老不贵嫩，贵瘦不贵肥，贵含不贵开"。南宋诗人范成大在《范村梅谱》中就曾说梅"以横斜疏瘦与老

fragrance. The ancient Chinese literati all spoke highly of the pleasant aroma of plum blossom. For instance, Lu Meipo, a well-known poet in the Southern Song Dynasty once extolled plum blossom to a great extent in his poem *Snow and Plum*, "Plum blossom and snowflake are competing for their beauty, neither of them will submit, which makes the poet stop writing and trying to find a fair remark. The plum blossom is less white than the snowflake, while the snowflake is beaten by the plum blossom on its aroma", which generally depicts that plum and snow vie for spring, and

枝怪奇者为贵"。可见"瘦"正是梅高雅脱俗之所在，以"瘦"为美正是宋人所推崇的，这种审美标准延续到明清时期。为了追求梅的"横斜疏瘦"，人们在培养梅花盆景时还会刻意砍掉梅树的正枝，培养斜侧的旁枝，去掉笔直的枝干，用铁丝和绳子将其枝干牵拉捆绑起来，使其生长得弯曲有致。这种人工雕琢的美到了清代末期，受到了不少追求自然美的文人的批评。

- 《白梅翠禽图》佚名（宋）
  Painting of White Plum Blossom and Kingfisher (Song Dynasty, 960-1279)

neither admit defeat; even poets put down brushes, hesitating to comment; to be fair, plum is inferior to snow, short of three-tenth white, yet snow is beaten by plum for lack of a whiff of scent. Besides, in order to highlight the unique fragrance to plum blossom, people also compared the blossom of peach or apricot with that of the plum blossom. Despite its glamour, the peach blossom has a fragrance that is somewhat too sweet for the literati and hence cannot match the faint and gentle aroma of the plum blossom. Lu You, a famous Chinese poet in the Southern Song Dynasty once related in his poem that compared with the ordinary peach and apricot blossom, he liked plum blossom better which so intoxicate him that a smell of it can spell him to sleep off spring. Another poet Lv Benzhong likewise sang highly of the plum blossom, saying that its fragrance is not for the vulgar nose, and only person of refined taste can relish it to the utmost. Actually in ancient China many women were named *Meixiang* (literally meaning the fragrance of the plum blossom), which might have something to do with their love of the aroma of plum blossom.

The standard applied by ancient literati to the appreciation of plum

• 《红梅图》吴昌硕
Red Plum Blossom,
by Wu Changshuo

其实在现实生活中，确实有一种梅花的枝干生来便具有这样的特点，这就是龙游梅。光听名字就可想象龙游梅的形态像蜿蜒的游龙，老干虬枝，扭曲有致，极尽苍劲盘曲之势。在江南，人们往往将龙游梅植于灰瓦粉墙之下的开阔处，倘若能细细品味那自然扭曲之态，人们会不由得赞叹它的百折不挠之美。

blossom can be summed up as Four Values, that is, to value sparsity rather than intricacy, to value the aged branch rather than the tender shoot, to value the skinny rather than the stout, and to value the bud rather than the full bloom. Fan Chengda, a Chinese poet in the Southern Song Dynasty once wrote in his *Book of Plum Trees* that the best plum blossom is that with crosswise, sparse, skinny,

与梅有关的传统吉祥图案

梅花主题的装饰图案产生于秦汉时期，明清以来成为人们最喜闻乐见的吉祥图案之一，广泛用于玉器、瓷器、雕刻、服饰、家具装饰等领域。

Traditional Auspicious Designs Related to Plum Blossom

Early in the Qin, Western Han and Eastern Han dynasties decorative designs had taken the plum blossom as one theme. Since the Ming and Qing dynasties it has become one of the most beloved auspicious designs and been widely used to ornament jade, porcelain, sculpture, clothing, furniture, etc.

踏雪寻梅

踏雪寻梅，常用来表达文人雅士赏爱风景、苦心作诗的情致，后来成为文人淡泊名利的象征，演绎为千古流传的佳话。

• 青花《踏雪寻梅》图罐（明）
Blue-and-white Porcelain Jar with Design of *Wandering amidst Snow in Search of Plum Blossom* (Ming Dynasty, 1368-1644)

Design of Wandering amidst Snow in Search of Plum Blossom

The design was often used to express the sentiment of the literati who loved the scenery and painstakinly composed poems. It later became a symbol of the noble spirit of the literati indifferent to fame and wealth, and is praised far and wide through the ages.

喜上眉梢

在中国民间，人们相信喜鹊是一种有灵性的鸟，能够向人报告喜讯。"喜上眉梢"这个成语的原意是喜悦的心情从眉眼上表现出来，人们以梅花谐音"眉"字，构成喜鹊飞上梅枝的图案，寓意喜事来临、喜从天降。

Design of Magpies in the Plum Branch

In the eyes of the folk Chinese, the magpie is an intelligent bird which is able to report good news to the people. This idiom originally means one's happiness can be traced from the facial looks, especially the curved eyes and brows. As the Chinese character that refers to eyebrow is a homonym of the character for plum, people usually use the design of magpies in the plum branch to signify the advent of good tidings or unexpected joy.

- 青花釉里红喜上梅梢纹方瓶（清）
Under-glazed Red Blue-and-white Square Vase with Design of Magpies in the Plum Branch (Qing Dynasty, 1616-1911)

- 黄地水墨梅花绶带鸟盖碗（近代）
Yellow-ground Lidded Bowl with Design of Ink Plum Blossom and Paradise Flycatchers (Modern Times)

- 北京北海撷秀亭喜上梅梢彩画
  Colored Painting of Magpies in the Plum Branch on the Xiexiu Pavilion at Beihai Park, Beijing

齐眉祝寿

　　齐眉祝寿图案由梅花和绶带鸟构成。据《后汉书》记载，东汉学者梁鸿与妻子孟光感情很好。每天用餐时，孟光都把放有饭菜的食案举到与眉毛同高的位置，递给梁鸿，以示恭敬。"举案齐眉"便成了夫妻恩爱的代称。齐眉祝寿就是根据这个故事而来。其中"梅"与"眉"谐音，绶带鸟的"绶"与"寿"字谐音，寓意夫妻恩爱、白头偕老。

Design of Plum Blossom and Paradise Flycatcher

　　This design consists of plum blossom and paradise flycatcher. According to records in the *History of the Later Han*, Liang Hong, a scholar in the Eastern Han Dynasty and his wife Meng Guang were quite devoted to each other. Every day at meals, Meng Guang would raise all wooden dishes to the height of his eyebrows to show

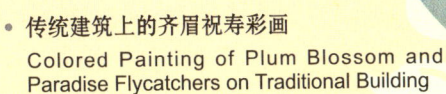

- 传统建筑上的齐眉祝寿彩画
  Colored Painting of Plum Blossom and Paradise Flycatchers on Traditional Building

respect before passing them to Liang Hong. From their story comes an idiom that lauds the genuine affection between wife and husband, and also the design that celebrates conjugal bliss. Here again the Chinese character for plum and that for eyebrow are homophonic, the Chinese character for paradise flycatcher also has a homonym that means longevity, hence this design is often used to depict happy marriage.

梅开五福

常见的梅花有五片花瓣，人们赋予其"福、禄、寿、喜、财"五种寓意。

Design of Plum Blossom's Five Blessings

The common plum blossom usually has five petals, and people lend them five implications, respectively good fortune, prosperity, longevity, joy and wealth.

- 山东潍坊年画《梅花开五福》
New Year Painting of *Plum Blossom's Five Blessings* in Weifang City, Shandong Province

• 青花劲梅纹花钵
Blue-and-white Floral Bowl with Design of Vigorous Plum

• 《古梅图轴》朱耷（清）
Painting Scroll of Ancient Plum, by Zhu Da (Qing Dynasty, 1616-1911)

aged and strange branches, from which we can see skinniness is exactly where the refined elegance of plum lies in and the skinny beauty is what the people in the Song Dynasty praise. This standard was sustained till the Ming and Qing dynasties. To achieve it, when cultivating plum blossom bonsais, people would deliberately cut off the main stems of the plum tree, and then nurture the offshoots, prune the upright limbs, use wires and ropes to pull its branches together so that it can bend with grace in an intriguing way. Towards the late Qing Dynasty, such artificial polished beauty was greatly criticized by many literati in pursuit of natural elegance.

Actually in real life, there is a kind of plum whose branches are born with these features, and that is tortuous plum. Its name has already to a certain extent suggested its posture winding like a moving dragon. The aged twigs curl yet retain elegance and vigor. In regions south of the Yangtze River, people usually plant the tortuous plum in an open place under the whitewashed wall of gray tiles. If time allows, just savor each of its natural twist, then you cannot help but marvel at its indomitable beauty that defies all setbacks.

说梅 Ode to the Plum Blossom

• 苏州狮子林中的老梅盆景（图片提供：图虫创意）
Bonsai of Aged Plum in the Lion Grove Garden, Suzhou City

梅妻鹤子

  如果要推选出中国古代最爱梅花的人，那么宋代的著名诗人林逋当仁不让。林逋（967—1028），浙江钱塘（今浙江杭州）人。他自幼好学，通晓经史，性格孤高自好，成年后隐居在杭州西湖。相传他一生没有出来做官，平时就喜欢坐着小船游览西湖美景，过着悠闲的日子。林逋一生未娶，最爱植梅养鹤，自谓"以梅为妻，以鹤为子"，人称"梅妻鹤子"。《山园小梅》是他最负盛名的代表诗作：

  众芳摇落独暄妍，占尽风情向小园。
  疏影横斜水清浅，暗香浮动月黄昏。
  霜禽欲下先偷眼，粉蝶如知合断魂。
  幸有微吟可相狎，不须檀板共金樽。

诗歌的大意是：园里的百花都已经凋残了，此时只有梅花生机勃勃，傲然盛开。朦胧的月光下，梅枝或横或斜，或密或疏，错落有致地倒映在清澈的水面上，夜色里、空气中飘散着一股淡淡的清香，若有若无。寒雀想飞落下来，先偷看了梅花一眼；蝴蝶如果知道梅花的美，定会销魂失魄。幸喜我能通过低声吟咏和梅花亲近，不用敲檀板唱歌、执金杯饮酒来欣赏它了。

诗中的"疏影横斜水清浅，暗香浮动月黄昏"两句，成功地描绘出梅花清幽香逸的风姿，被誉为千古咏梅绝唱，以致使"疏影""暗香"后来成为梅花的代称。林逋痴于梅花，赏于梅花，知音于梅花，将梅的姿态写得入木三分。时至今日，人们还能透过诗句去领略梅花独有的美。

- 《梅妻鹤子》潘振镛（清）
  Taking Plum Blossom as Wife and Cranes as Children, by Pan Zhenyong (Qing Dynasty, 1616-1911)

Taking Plum Blossom as Wife and Cranes as Children

If to select one from the ancients who loves plum blossom best, Lin Bu (967-1029), the remarkable poet in the Northern Song Dynasty, really deserves the title. He was born in Qiantang (today's Hangzhou), Zhejiang Province. Ever since childhood, he showed a studious bent, mastered the classics as well as history, yet because of a lofty disposition and great self-respect, for much of his adulthood he lived in quiet seclusion by the West Lake in Hangzhou. According to the legend, he never started the official career at all, and instead spent his lifetime sitting in the boat and surrendering himself to the beauty of the West Lake. He led a life like an immortal in earthly paradise. He never married, devoted all his love to plum trees and cranes, and even claimed the plum blossom as his wife, and the cranes as his children. One of his most famous poems is *Little Plum Blossom of Hill Garden*:

Bloom solely despite others' withering,
It flourishes beautifully and vigorously.
In water reflects those randomly stretched branches,
Wisps of aroma linger in the night air.
Birds want to steal a glance at her,
Butterfly will be obsessed if witnessing her beauty.
How fortunate I can approach her through chanting,
Instead of singing songs and drinking wines.

It can be translated as follows: when everything in the garden has faded, the plum blossom alone shine forth proudly in full bloom. Its scattered shadows fall sidelong on the clear water or dense or sparse, whereas its subtle scent pervades the moonlit dusk. Birds peep again before they land, and butterflies would faint if they but knew the beauty of wintry blossom. Thankfully I can approach them in whispered verse and need no sounding hardwood clappers or a golden wine cup to feel their sweetness.

The second line of the poem successfully depicts the graceful posture as well as delicate fragrance of the plum blossom, and is regarded as a masterpiece of its kind throughout the ages. Both the scattered shadows and the subtle fragrance later become synonyms for plum blossom. Lin Bu is crazy about plum blossom, appreciates and even regards it as bosom friend; hence his depiction of the postures is direct and penetrating. Even today we are able to relish the unique beauty of plum blossom through his verse.

> 梅之精神

梅的花瓣柔弱轻盈，清香袭人，枝条却是苍劲曲折，粗犷遒劲，高雅精致的花朵与老干虬枝形成了极强烈的对比。或许正是梅花的自然属性与古人的精神追求相契合，梅在中国人心目中便不再只是简单的植物品种，而成为有着众多意象的化身了。

梅花盛开于寒风凛冽、大雪纷飞的冬季，当百花凋谢、树木枯萎时，是梅花让人们看到了清冷中的一丝暖意，它传达着春天的消息。元代杨维桢赞其"万花敢向雪中出，一树独先天下春"。一个"敢"字，把梅花这种敢为天下先的勇猛精神表露无遗，而"先"字，则说出了梅花是最早报春的使者，把梅那种不惧严寒、乐观向上

> Spirit of Plum Blossom

Plum blossom bears delicate lithe petals and soft fragrance, whereas the aged branches appear rather vigorous with twists and turns, hence striking is the contrast between the elegant flowers and the rough branches. Perhaps it is precisely because the natural attributes of the plum blossom correspond to the spiritual pursuits of the ancients, that the plum blossom is no longer regarded simply as a plant in the eyes of the Chinese, but becomes the embodiment of numerous virtues.

While all other flowers and trees either wither or fade in their beauty, the plum blossom alone blossom in snowy winter against the chilly wind, allowing people a trace of warmth in the cold by a message from spring. Yang Weizhen, a Chinese poet in the Yuan Dynasty once eulogized the valor of plum blossom that

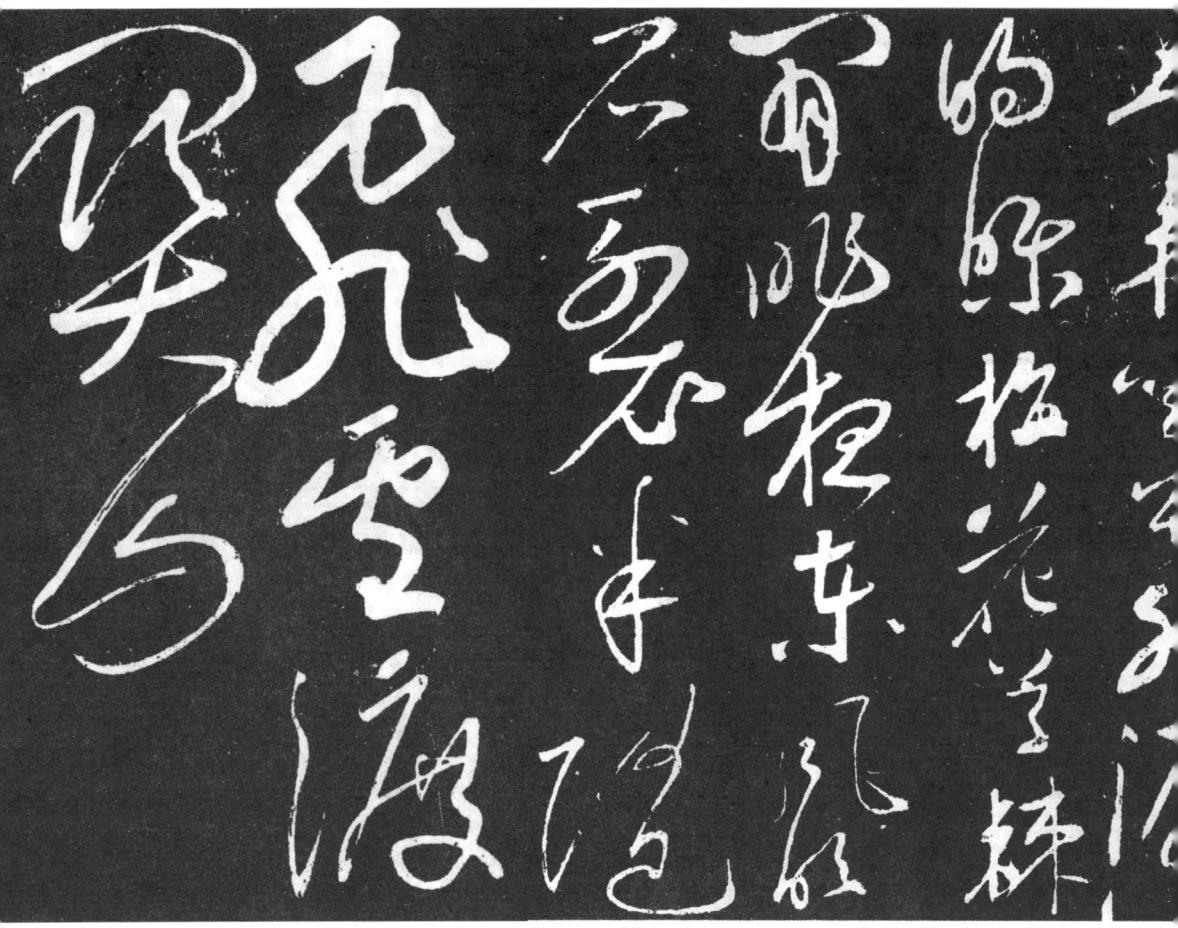

- 《梅花诗帖》苏轼【局部】（北宋）

"春来幽谷水潺潺，的皪梅花草棘间。昨夜东风吹石裂，半随飞雪渡关山。"这首《梅花诗》写于苏轼被贬湖北黄州期间。当时正值大雪，苏轼偶然在山岭的荒草间发现了一株绽开的梅花，深受触动，用草书写了这首梅花诗。前两行平稳自如，后几行笔势突变，以狂草收笔，观者可以感受到苏轼在书写时情感的变化。

Part of the Manuscript of *Plum Blossom Poem*, by Su Shi (Northern Song Dynasty, 960-1127)

This poem was written during Su Shi's exile in Huangzhou, Hubei Province. It can be literally translated as, "Chanting spring creek through the hushed valley fares; in bushes of thorn, plum blossom in glittering glam they share; last night an east gale surged, with stone-shattering force; half the petals, with blowing snow, o'er the border they dared." Actually it was snowing at that time, and Su Shi happened to find a blooming plum amid the mountain weeds. Deeply moved, he wrote this poem in cursive style. The first two lines ran in a poised and smooth manner, whereas in the later ones he suddenly shifted the stroke, and ended with a remarkable flourish of the wild cursive draft. Thence we can feel Su Shi's emotional changes in the course of composition.

的精神表现得淋漓尽致。梅花能够忍受冬天的严酷,在酷寒的环境下,枝条上包裹着冰,冰又包着花朵,但风雪过后,梅花依然继续开放,还有哪一种花能够做得到呢?

北宋大文学家苏轼对梅花更有"玉雪为骨冰为魂"的赞美之语,梅花所代表的是一种敢于抗争的精神,这种抗争精神与君子的一种人格精神相契合。中国的儒家文化讲究"修身、齐家、治国、平天下",修身是君子的起点,"治国、平天下"的大任是其落脚点。于是君子自强不息、锐意进取,时刻准备着"鞠躬尽瘁,死而后已"。他们不畏困难艰辛,怀着"虽九死犹未悔"的信念,永不放弃,敢于在危难之时挺身而出的大无畏精神和品格,与不畏严寒、隐忍高洁的梅花非常相似。

南宋陆游有一首脍炙人口之作《卜算子·咏梅》:"驿外断桥边,寂寞开无主。已是黄昏独自愁,更着风和雨。无意苦争春,一任群芳妒,零落成泥碾作尘,只有香如故。"这首千古绝唱的大意是:驿站外面残破的断桥边,一株

dare to be the first, even if it means to burst in snow, and precede all others as harbinger of spring. Hence the defying spirit and blithe optimism are all too thoroughly revealed. Plum blossom can endure harsh winter. Even in the bitter cold when the branches and flowers are wrapped in ice, it still blossom after the howling blizzard. Indeed any flower else can do so likewise as well?

Su Shi, the great man of letters in the Northern Song Dynasty exalted the plum blossom above all others, claiming its bones are of snow, and its soul is of ice. In other words, the plum blossom represents a daring spirit to fight against, a spirit that contributes to a gentleman's nobility and sustains one's nationality. Chinese Confucian culture pays great attention to self-cultivation, regulating the family, then governing the state, and finally giving peace to the world. Self-cultivation is where a gentleman should start his accomplishment, whereas state-management and peace-making is his responsibility, his end. Therefore it is often said that gentlemen should exert self-reliance, constantly strive to forge ahead, always be ready to go all out for it despite their life and regardless of any difficulty. Also they must have the faith

寒梅悄然开放，在黄昏里独自寂寞忧愁，任寒风吹冷雨浇。它并不是有意争当第一个报春的使者，但却一再被群芳嫉妒猜疑。梅花的花瓣虽飘落地面被碾成了灰尘，但是它的清香却并未消失，仍留在空

in heart that for national glory I do not regret to die ten thousand times, and dare to come forward in times of distress with perseverance and courage. Their undaunted spirit is very similar to that of the plum blossom which defy any cold and burst forth a noble beauty by a remarkable feat of endurance.

Lu You, in the Southern Song Dynasty, once wrote an ode to the plum blossom, *Ode to Plum Blossom; to the Tune of "Song of Divination"*, which enjoyed great popularity, "Along the broken bridge outside the post, I am wandering lonesome. It's already the dusk, and with the wind and rain. The plum blossom doesn't mean to stand out for showing its beauty, however envied by all the other flowers. Despite its petals drifting down to the ground, the aroma is still the same." It literally means near the broken bridge, outside the post-house a flower blooms, lonely and disoriented. Saddened by her solitude in the falling dusk, she is assailed by wind and rain. Let other

- 《红梅图》王雪涛（近代）
Painting Scroll of Red Plum Blossom, by Wang Xuetao (Modern Times)

气中。词中句句写梅，亦是句句自状，其中梅花就是诗人自己的化身。最后一句"零落成泥碾作尘，只有香如故"，字字铿锵，掷地有声。

南北朝的诗人陆凯有一首著名的《赠范晔》，被誉为古来第一首咏梅之作：

折梅逢驿使，寄于陇头人。
江南无所有，聊赠一枝春。

flowers be envious. She craves not Spring for herself alone. Her petals may fall to the ground and be crushed into dust, but her fragrance will endure in the air. The poem is dedicated to the plum blossom, yet the poet embedded himself in each line of it. In fact, the plum blossom has incarnated his spirit. Especially in the last line where every word rings sonorously.

- 陆游像
  Portrait of Lu You

- 蓝缎地蝴蝶梅花图案女衬衣（清）
  Blue Satin Blouse with Design of Butterflies and Plum Blossom
  (Qing Dynasty, 1616-1911)

诗句的大意是：我折梅花时恰好遇到信使，于是将花寄给你这个身在陇头的好友。江南没有什么好东西可以表达我的情感，姑且送给你一枝报春的梅花吧。诗人与友人远离千里，难以相见，只能靠驿使互递问候。首句一个"逢"字，看似不经意，由驿使而想到友人，

Lu Kai, a famous poet in the Southern and Northern dynasties, once wrote a poem titled *To Fan Ye*, which is known as the very first ode to plum blossom since ancient times, "I encountered the messenger while breaking the plum branch, so send this to you my dear friend. I have nothing to express my feelings to you, only

▸ 一枝春梅
A branch of plum blossom in spring

青花矾红描金画卷开光竹梅纹盘（清）
Blue-and-white Plate with Framing Decorations of Iron-red and Gold-lining Bamboo and Plum Blossom (Qing Dynasty, 1616-1911)

于是寄梅问候，却体现了诗人对朋友的殷殷挂念。江南并不是一无所有，有的正是诗人的诚挚情怀和深深祝福，这一切全凝聚在小小的一枝梅花上了。

此后，"折梅赠远"就成为一个著名的典故，而"一枝春"也成为梅花的代称之一了。后世许多文人都用"折梅"来表达思念之情。如北宋词人秦观在《踏莎行》中的名句："驿寄梅花，鱼传尺素，砌成此

this branch of plum blossom to present you as a sign of spring." The gist of the poem goes that,"I happened to meet the messenger when I broke a plum twig, so I sent the plum blossom to you, my friend in Longtou; I found nothing good in South China that can convey my feelings, and for the moment being, please accept this branch of spring as a token of my longing for you." Thousands of miles away from each other, they can only rely on the messenger to exchange greetings. The word "happen" in the first line assumes a careless attitude, yet it reflects deep solicitude of the caring poet, who through the messenger immediately thought of his friend and then sent plum blossom to greet him. In fact, the regions south of the Yangtze River do have something good-sincere feelings and deep blessings from our poet, and all are condensed in this little branch of plum blossom.

Henceforward, breaking a plum branch as a gift to friends afar develops from a much-told tale to a well-known literary allusion. "A branch of spring" also becomes one synonym for plum blossom. Later many scholars used "breaking plum" to express their longing. For instance, Qin Guan, a Chinese poet

恨无重数。"大意是：驿站寄来了梅花，以鱼形函套传递书信，越是收到来自朋友的慰藉，越是增添重重愁绪。南宋诗人刘克庄也有"轻烟小雪孤行路，折剩梅花寄一枝"之句。在这些诗句里，梅已经成为一种情感的载体，一种思念的象征。

in the Northern Song Dynasty once wrote a poem to the *Tune of Walking through the Sedge-grass*. One much quoted line is related to our subject, "The post-house sent a branch of plum blossom and a fish-shaped letter; such a solace from friend rather multiplied my sorrow, for it triggered my longing for him." Liu Kezhuang, a noted poet in the Southern Song Dynasty related something alike in his verse, "In the flurries of snow I walked alone; then I broke a remaining plum branch and sent it to my friend." From these poems we can see that the plum blossom has already become a carrier of emotion, an emblem of longing.

- 白玉镂雕梅花纹帽正（明）

帽正是古代人帽子上的装饰物，又叫"帽准"，俗称"一块玉"。帽正在明清两代非常流行，多为玉石、玛瑙等材料制成，有圆形、方形，缀缝在帽子前面，戴上时正对鼻尖。

White Jade Hollowed-out Headpiece Decoration in Shape of Plum Blossom (Ming Dynasty, 1368-1644)

Maozheng or *Maozhun* is a decoration applied by the ancients to their headpieces, also known as one-piece jade. It was very popular in the Ming and Qing dynasties and mostly made of jade, agate and other precious materials. It can be round or square in shape, usually sewn in the front of the headpiece. One should align it with the tip of the nose when wearing.

赏梅胜地邓尉山

邓尉山位于江苏省苏州市西南部，相传东汉太尉邓禹曾隐居于此，因而得名。这里自古是中国的赏梅胜地之一，有"邓尉梅花甲天下"之称。清初一位巡抚名叫宋荦，他来到邓尉山时，看到绵绵山丘之上数十万株梅花竞相开放，宛若海洋，微寒的空气中流溢着若有若无的清香，远远望去，遍地落花，如同茫茫白雪，于是触景生情，当下题写了"香雪海"三字，令人镌刻在崖壁上。相传，清康熙皇帝曾三次到邓尉山赏梅。乾隆皇帝六次南巡，都曾到邓尉山探梅，还留下了赏梅诗作，使得"香雪海"名扬天下。

Dengwei Mountain-Famous Resort of Plum Blossom

Dengwei Mountain is located in the southwest of Suzhou City, Jiangsu Province. It is said that Deng Yu, a military official of the Eastern Han Dynasty once lived here in seclusion, so the mountain was named after him. Ever since ancient times it has been one of the famous resorts in China for plum blossom and even noted as the No. 1 Scenic Spot under Heaven of its kind. In the early Qing Dynasty, a governor named Song Luo came here. He saw on the rolling hills hundred thousands of plum in blossom. Everywhere was an ocean of flowers. In the slightly cold air flowed their faint fragrance. Far into the distance, all ground was covered with fallen petals white as powdery snow. So moved by the occasion, Song Luo instantly wrote three characters *Xiang Xue Hai*, meaning a sea of snowy plum blossom and had they engraved on the cliff. According to another legend, Emperor Kangxi of the Qing Dynasty had come to Dengwei Mountain thrice for its plum blossom. Emperor Qianlong toured to South China altogether six times and each time would not miss the plum blossom here. Besides, both of them have left poems on plum blossom, hence rendering the *Xiang Xue Hai* legendary all over the world.

邓尉山的"香雪海"（图片提供：CFP）
Xiang Xue Hai in Dengwei Mountain

> 墨梅暗香

自古以来，梅花常出现在画家的绘画作品中，它与兰、竹、菊一起被人称为"四君子"。历代画家为了更好地表现梅花的风神韵味，可谓苦心孤诣。

据画史记载，在南北朝时期就有人画梅了，到了北宋，画梅已经形成了一种风气。据元朝画家王冕《竹斋集》记载，北宋哲宗时，画梅比较有名的是仲仁。仲仁酷爱梅花，在其居住的屋边种植了数株梅花，每当梅花盛开时，他甚至会将自己的床移至梅树之下，吟咏终日。就是这位痴于梅花的仲仁创造了"墨梅"这一独特画法，他画梅花不赋颜色，仅用水墨的浓淡深浅来表现。据说在一个月明星稀的夜晚，仲仁就寝前不经意间看见窗外

> Delicate Fragrance of Ink Plum Blossom

Since ancient times, plum blossom has often appeared in paintings, which together with orchid, bamboo and chrysanthemum refer to as the Four Gentlemen. In order to catch the natural grace of plum blossom, painters of all generations have contributed painstaking efforts.

According to the painting history, early in the Southern and Northern dynasties artists already began to draw plum blossom. When it came to the Northern Song Dynasty (960-1127), plum painting prevailed in fashion. Based on the records in Wang Mian's (a famous Chinese painter in the Yuan Dynasty) *Collections of the Bamboo-House*, the famous plum painter in the Northern Song Dynasty was Zhong Ren who lived during the reign of Emperor Zhezong. He had a strong affinity for plum blossom. He planted many plum

《墨梅》张大千（现代）
Ink Plum Blossom, by Zhang Daqian (Modern Times)

梅花的影子照在纸窗上，疏影横斜，十分可爱。于是他拿起毛笔在纸上模拟着梅花的影子画起来，横竖点染，不一会儿便将这窗上的梅影勾勒了出来，于是便创造出了这种仅用水墨晕染而成的墨梅。北宋大书法家黄庭坚曾赞叹仲仁的墨梅"如嫩寒清晓行孤山篱落间，但欠香耳"，除了闻不到梅花的香气，这简直就是活生生的梅花啊。

古人认为，并不是人人都能画好梅花，画梅人必须有"梅气骨"，即画家需要有高尚的情操和洁身自好的品格，正所谓："画梅

trees in his residence and when they started to bloom, he would even move his bed under the plum trees, chanting them all day long. It was exactly this infatuated Zhong Ren who initiated the unique painting style of ink plum blossom. That is, he did not color the flowers but employed the various shades of ink and wash to present their natural beauty. As the story runs, on a moonlit night Zhong Ren was about to go to bed when accidentally he saw the sparse shadows of outside plum blossom reflected on the paper window. They were either transverse or oblique, all cute in posture. So he picked up a brush and began to imitate their shadows on paper. By a variety of strokes, horizontal or vertical, together with a few touches, he soon outlined the plum shadows, and hence created ink plum blossom which just as its name indicates, is painted in ink and wash alone. Huang Tingjian, a great Chinese calligrapher in the Northern Song Dynasty once highly praised Zhong Ren's ink plum blossom, saying that except for the aroma, it was true to life in every inch.

The ancients believed that not everyone could paint plum blossom well. A good plum painter must have

须有梅气骨，人与梅花一样清。"宋朝有位擅长画梅的画家扬无咎（1097—1169），被人誉为"墨梅擅天下，身后寸纸千金"。扬无咎年轻时居住的地方有一棵"大如数间屋"的老梅树，苍皮藓斑，繁花如簇。他经常对着梅树临画写生，甚得梅花真趣。在梅花的画法上，他既有对前人的继承，又有自己独特的感悟，形成了自己的画法。他一生都生活在民间，画名却不胫而走。还有一个传说，南宋时宫中人曾偶然将一幅扬无咎画的梅花拿出来悬挂，竟然引来蜜蜂和蝴蝶围绕飞舞，高宗皇帝一看颇为吃惊，急诏扬无咎进宫，奈何当时扬无咎已经病故了。

元代画家王冕集爱梅、咏梅、植梅、画梅于一身。他晚年隐居于会稽（今浙江绍兴）的九里山中，植梅千株，并将自己所住的房屋命名为"梅花屋"。他擅画墨梅，笔下的墨梅繁花密蕊，劲健有力，给人以热烈蓬勃、积极向上之感。王冕不仅画墨梅，有时还另辟蹊径，以胭脂色画"没骨梅"，更是别具风格。他的《墨梅》诗名扬天下：

the spirit of plum himself, or in other words, the artist should have noble sentiment, morally as pure as the plum blossom. Yang Wujiu was a talented plum painter in the Song Dynasty, who was so distinguished that each of his ink plum paintings was a priceless treasure. In youth Yang Wujiu lived beside an aged plum tree as huge as several rooms, with dark green mossy bark and clusters of blossom. He often sketched this plum tree and in the course of time caught the very spirit of the plum blossom. In terms of painting style, he inherited from his predecessors on the one hand and showed unique insight to develop his own individual style on the other. While all lifetime he spent among the folk, his fame in painting spread like wildfire. Another legend has that, one of Yang Wujiu's plum blossom paintings happened to be hung out in the court of the Southern Song Dynasty, which unexpectedly attracted bees and butterflies to fly around. Emperor Gaozong was so amazed that he sent for Yang Wujiu immediately. Yet unfortunate was he, for our painter had already died of a disease.

Wang Mian, a remarkable Chinese painter in the Yuan Dynasty in fact embodied all that is related to plum

- **扬无咎《四梅图》（宋）**

  扬无咎在仲仁画梅的基础上又进一步发展了墨梅画法，以双钩法来画梅花，使梅花更显纯洁高雅。现藏于故宫博物院的《四梅图》便是他墨梅的代表作。从图里的自跋中可知，作者创作的初衷是要完成一位朋友的命题："画梅四枝，一未开，一欲开，一盛开，一将残，仍各赋词一首。"《四梅图》分为四部分，画梅花"未开"，在疏枝斜干上突出描绘了花苞，以少胜多；画梅花"欲开"，在枝干上布了些整朵梅花，花瓣清晰，却不露花蕊，以求含蕴；画梅花"盛开"，则极写其绽放的美态；画梅花"将残"，则凋落飘零，枝上的残梅也是蕊托外露，已无一瓣可寻。四段梅花图，将梅花由盛而衰的过程表现得淋漓尽致，不经过仔细揣摩观察，是无法具备如此准确传神的表现力的。

Four Stages of Plum Blossom, by Yang Wujiu (Song Dynasty, 960-1279)

Yang Wujiu inherited and further developed the legacy of Zhong Ren in ink plum blossom painting. He applied the double-stroke technique-which uses two lines to contour circled petals and then colors within the outline-hence rendering the plum blossom purer and more elegant. *Four Stages of Plum Blossom* now stored in the Palace Museum is his masterpiece of ink plum blossom. From the postscript in the scroll we can see that his original intention was to complete a friend's assignment, "Draw four plum branches, one is still in bud, one is about to bloom, one in full blossom, one about to fade and all have a poem as inscription." The painting consists of four sections. The first highlights the plum buds on the sparse inclined spray, though a few yet quite prominent. The second depicts a plum about to bloom. The artist paints some flowers on the branch with clear-cut petals but no protruding stamens so as to achieve an implicit effect and retain some connotation. The third has a plum spray in full blossom, exalting its natural beauty to the utmost. And the last section is devoted to its final stage when the flowers are fading, falling; even those still left on the branch have exposed stamens with no petals. *Four Stages of Plum Blossom* thoroughly illustrates the whole process of plum blossom from flourishing to decline. Only by a careful observation and study can a painter bring out an image so vivid, accurate and expressive.

我家洗砚池头树，朵朵花开淡墨痕。
不用人夸好颜色，只流清气满乾坤。

诗句的大意是：我家洗砚池边的梅花树，花开朵朵，都是用淡淡的墨汁点染而成。它不需要别人夸奖颜色好，只要散发清香之气，充满天地之间。这首诗生动地传达出了梅花的清肌傲骨，寄托了文人雅士孤高傲岸的情怀。

王冕的存世绘画名作有《墨梅图》，此画写倒垂梅花，虽然小枝条从各方旁逸而出，却不改下垂之主势，枝干主次分明；以双钩法勾花，以野逸自如的笔致来描绘梅花，倍显勃勃生机。

晚清书画家吴昌硕也是酷爱梅花之人，自称"苦铁道人梅知己"。有一年冬天，鹅毛大雪把他家园中花开最盛的老梅压折了，落在邻家园内。吴昌硕十分惋惜，于是铺开纸画了一枝老梅。他还曾在一幅《墨梅图》中题诗道："人间干净地无多，欲结孤根奈如何？写入图中悬素壁，春风日日在岩阿。"大意是，人间的土地没有多少干净的地方，梅花的根要扎在哪

blossom. He loved it, lauded the plum in odes, planted and also painted it. In his later years he lived in seclusion at Mountain Jiuli in Kuaiji (today's Shaoxing City, Zhejiang Province), planted numerous plum trees, and even named his residence "Plum Blossom House". He specialized at ink plum blossom, pioneering a dense style that is bold and vigorous with massive flowers, all giving a passionate, vibrant and positive sense. Wang Mian not only excelled at ink plum painting, but blazed a new trail from time to time. For instance, he applied rouge color to painting plum blossom of the boneless style which is really unique and interesting. His poem *Ink Plum* is also world-famous:

The plum tree standing by the side of my inkslab-washing pond;
All the blooming blossom are tinged by light ink.
They don't need the praise from others;
Only want to leave wisps of aroma lingering in the world.

It can be translated as follows: by the pond where I clean brushes and ink stones stand several plum trees that bear pale-dark

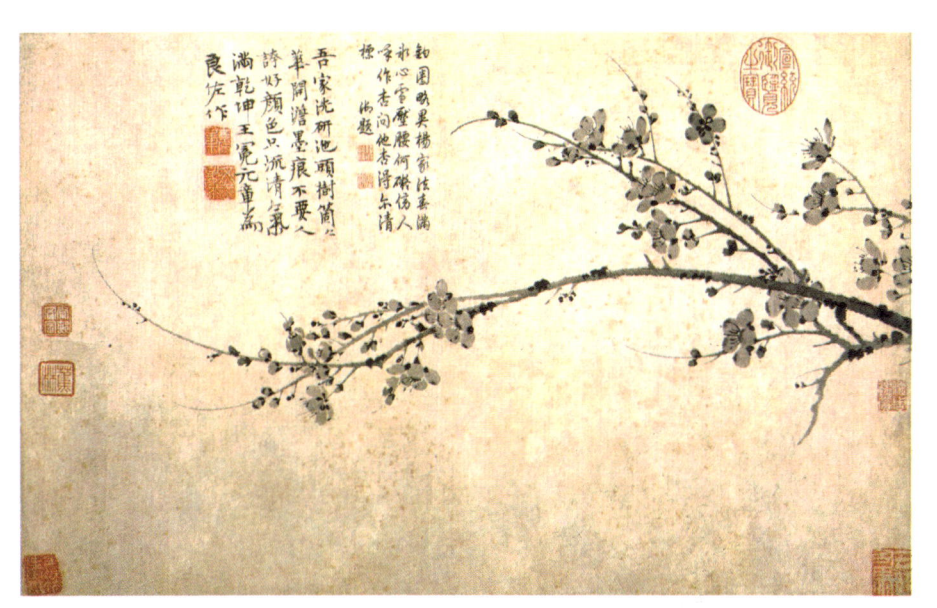

• 《墨梅图》王冕（元）
Ink Plum Blossom, by Wang Mian (Yuan Dynasty, 1206-1368)

里呢？只好把梅花写到图画中，悬到墙上，才能使其免受污秽之苦。

吴昌硕凭借浑厚的书法功底，在画梅时融入书法大篆的笔法，他将自己所画的梅花称为"扫梅"。

"扫"字，有出笔迅速、果断之意，他笔下的墨梅呈现出一种重起轻收的枯墨干擦的效果。他不仅画墨梅，还喜欢用朱砂、洋红点红梅，颜色虽然炽烈，但是浑厚的书法运笔硬如钢铁且见风骨，故而深受人们喜爱。

blossom as if tinged with light ink. They do not care compliment of fair color, leaving only a faint fragrance to permeate the vast universe. This poem vividly depicts the pure and lofty character of the plum blossom and also reveals the nobility of the literati who stand aloof from the worldly affairs.

Ink Plum Blossom Painting is one of Wang Mian's surviving masterpieces. This scroll mainly depicts a downward hanging plum. Although offshoots reach out from both sides, the tree still keeps a drooping tendency. The major and lesser branches remain distinctive. The dense blossom are outlined in double strokes and hence gain a natural elegance of considerable vitality.

Wu Changshuo, a Chinese calligrapher and painter in late Qing Dynasty, was also keen on plum blossom, and even claimed the plum as his bosom friend. One winter, the most flourishing aged plum in his garden was broke down by the heavy snow and fell in his neighbor's. Wu Changshuo felt so sorry about it that he took out a piece of paper and immediately painted an old plum. For one *Ink Plum Blossom Painting* he even inscribed a poem to the effect that, "There isn't much clean space in the human world, so where can the plum take root that cherishes purity so much? I find no way but to paint and then hang it on the wall. Hence it can avoid the worldly filth."

Due to solid calligraphic skills, Wu Changshuo integrated the large seal script into his paintings of plum blossom and even jokingly called it "Swept Plum Blossom" which precisely refers to his rapid and decisive strokes. The ink plum blossom under his brush begins in heavy stroke and ends lightly with a special

- 《墨梅图》吴昌硕（清）

  吴昌硕画梅，善于画出梅的不同形态，用以表达人的不同情感。他说，有的梅花秀丽如美人，有的梅花孤冷如老僧，有的梅花坚贞如诤臣，也有的梅花孤傲如侠客。

  Painting of Ink Plum Blossom, by Wu Changshuo (Qing Dynastay, 1616-1911)

  Wu Changshuo is expert in painting ink plum blossom of different forms to express different emotions. He said, some plum flowers are as elegant as a beauty, some lonely and cold like an old monk, some faithful as a loyal minister who will give forthright admonition, and others can be so aloof like a chivalrous knight.

吴昌硕旧照
Old Photo of Wu Changshuo

effect as if rubbed by dry ink. He was not only good at ink plum painting, but liked using vermilion or magenta to mark red plum blossom, which, though blazing in color, yet carries strength hard as iron because of his vigorous calligraphic strokes and hence enjoy great popularity.

《茗具梅花图》吴昌硕（清）
Painting of Tea Set and Plum Blossom, by Wu Changshuo (Qing Dynasty, 1616-1911)

五大古梅

楚梅：在湖北荆州市沙市区章华寺内，相传为春秋时期楚国国君楚灵王所植，至今已有2500多年，是中国现存最早的古梅。

晋梅：在湖北黄冈市黄梅县"江心古寺"遗址处，据《黄梅县志》记载，这株梅乃东晋名僧支遁亲手所栽，每年冬春两季开花，又称"二度梅"。

隋梅：在浙江天台山国清寺大殿东侧的小院中，距今已1400多年，曾数度枯萎，又死而复荣，花开满枝。

唐梅：在浙江杭州超山风景区的大明堂院内，相传植于唐朝开元年间，花开季节，梅花万朵，香飘数里，被誉为"超山之宝"。

宋梅：也在浙江超山风景区，种于报慈寺前。一般梅花都是五瓣，这株宋梅却花开六瓣，十分稀奇。这株宋梅挺拔苍劲，花繁枝茂，年产梅子三四十公斤。

Five Ancient Plum Trees

Chu Plum. The Chu Plum is housed in Zhanghua Temple, Shashi District, Jinzhou City, Hubei Province. According to the legend, it was planted by King Ling of State Chu during the Spring and Autumn Period (770 B.C.-476 B.C.). It is over 2500 years old and known as the earliest plum tree ever extant up to the present.

Jin Plum. It resides in the site of the ancient Jiangxin Temple, Huangmei County, Huanggang City, Hubei Province. Based on the county annals, this plum was planted by Zhidun himself, a noted monk in the Eastern Jin Dynasty (317-420). It flowers in both winter and spring, hence also known as "Plum Blossoming Twice".

Sui Plum. It grows at the eastern yard of Guoqing Temple, Tiantai Mountain, Zhejiang Province for more than 1400 years. For several times the plum withered, but always revived after a while and flourished in blossom.

Tang Plum. It still thrives in the yard of Damingtang in Chaoshan Scenic Area, Hangzhou City, Zhejiang Province. The legend has that it was planted during the Period Kaiyuan in the Tang Dynasty (713-741). When the plum flowers, thousands of blossom contend in beauty, and one can scent the fragrance even ten thousand miles away. It is therefore honored as "Gem of the Chaoshan Mountain".

Song Plum. It lives in front of the Baoci Temple also in Chaoshan Scenic Area, Zhejiang Province. Common plum blossom all have five petals, whereas this one surprisingly has six which is really rare. Besides, this Song Plum grows upright and vigorous with masses of flowers and dense branches, yielding 30 or 40 kilograms of plums every year.

说兰
Ode to the Orchid

　　兰花生于深谷，花色淡雅，含蓄内敛又有幽香清远，宛若空谷佳人一般高洁脱俗，后来便被儒家文化视为君子修道立德，不因穷困而变节的高贵品格的代表。

　　在汉语的词汇中，"兰"为美好的代称。人们用"兰章"来形容美好的文辞；用"兰室"来形容高雅的居室；用"兰藻"来形容美好的语言；用"兰客"形容品德高尚的朋友；用"义结金兰"形容因友情契合而结为兄弟。

Born in the deep valley, the orchid is quiet and elegant in color, reserved in temperament, and with a faint aroma that can flow afar. Always it gives an air of refined nobility like a lonely beauty living in deep seclusion. Later the Confucian culture incorporated this image to analogize the noble character of a gentleman who will not lose moral principle even in destitution.

In Chinese vocabulary, the character orchid becomes a synonym for fineness. People use orchid verse to describe beautiful proses; use orchid room to describe a tasteful living room; use orchid words to describe beautiful diction; and use orchid guest to describe a virtuous friend, sometimes even as token of firm friendship between two individuals who have become sworn brothers.

> 兰之品赏

兰花，多年生地生常绿草本植物。根簇生，为菌根，呈绳索状，根茎短，形成假鳞茎状。兰花的叶子细长，多为剑形或者带形，革质，多弧状弯曲，春季开花，气味清香，是深受中国人喜爱的传统花卉之一。

宋代出现了关于兰花的专著。南宋的赵时庚于1233年写成的《金漳兰谱》，可以说是中国现存最早的一部研究兰花的著作。此书分三卷，对30多个品种的兰花的形态特征作了简述。宋末元初的画家赵孟坚所绘的《春兰图》，被认为是现存最早的兰花名画。

明清两代，对兰花的栽培与欣赏进入了鼎盛时期。随着兰花品种的不断增加，栽培经验的日益丰

> Appreciation of Orchid

Orchid is a perennial and terrestrial evergreen herb. The root is a clustered rope-like mycorrhiza with short rootstalk of pseudobulb. The leaves are slender, mostly sword-shaped or band-shaped, leathery in texture, and bend like an arc. The orchid usually flowers in spring with a faint fragrance. It is one of the traditional flowers that are deeply beloved by the Chinese.

There had appeared specific works on orchid studies in the Song Dynasty (960-1279). For instance, Zhao Shigeng, a noted Chinese in the Southern Song Dynasty wrote *Manuals on Jinzhang Orchid* in 1233, the first book extant in China that studies orchidology systematically. The book is divided into three volumes and briefly introduces the morphological features of more than 30 varieties of orchid. *Spring Orchid*

• 春兰
Cymbidium Goeringii

富，兰花已成为上至士大夫下至平民百姓都十分喜爱的花卉。有关兰花的书籍、画册、诗作层出不穷，瓷器、雕刻等工艺品上的兰花图案也日渐增多。清代时浙江嘉兴人许霁和嗜兰成癖，又善画兰，具有丰富的养兰、赏兰经验，他在写于1856年的《兰蕙同心录》中详细讲述了植兰的知识、兰花品种的识别和分类方法等内容，全书记载兰花品种57个，还附有白描

by Zhao Mengjian, a celebrated painter living in the late Southern Song Dynasty and the early Yuan Dynasty, is well-known as the earliest extant orchid painting.

In the Ming and Qing dynasties, the cultivation and appreciation of orchid entered its golden age. As the varieties of orchid got increased and its cultivation experience accumulated, orchid became wildly popular both among the noble scholars and the common people. Relevant books, paintings and poems

图。后世爱兰者皆奉此书为经典，誉为兰花"诸谱之冠"。

兰花品种很多，依其生活形态，可分为附生兰（着生兰）和地生兰两大类，主要以地生兰为主。地生兰生长在有机质土壤中，茎叶比较薄软，根较细小，伸展于土壤中，不耐干旱。中国传统兰花常见的品种有春兰、蕙兰、建兰、寒兰、墨兰五种，其共同点是兰叶较为修长，花朵偏小，气味幽香。

• 一茎多花的蕙兰
Cymbidium Faberi with Many Flowers on one Stalk.

emerged in large numbers. Moreover, orchid was increasingly adopted as a pattern to decorate porcelain, sculpture and other craftworks. Xu Naihe of the Qing Dynasty who lived in Shaoxing City, Zhejiang Province indeed became an orchid addict. He was not only good at painting orchid, but also expert in cultivation and appreciation. In his *Handbook on Orchid* written in 1856, Xu gave a detailed account of his orchid planting experience, how to identify and classify orchid species, etc. The book records altogether 57 varieties of orchid with illustrations in line drawing. Later orchid lovers all regard this book as crown of all classics of its kind.

Orchid is rich in species and in terms of different lifestyles, it can be divided into epiphytic orchid and terrestrial orchid, and mainly terrestrial orchid. The terrestrial orchid grows in organic soil. The stem and leaves are thin and soft, the small root does not extend deep in the earth and hence is not draught-enduring. The common classical Chinese orchid include cymbidium goeringii, cymbidium faberi, cymbidium ensifolium, crybidium kankan and cymbidium sinense. All have slender leaves, small flowers and faint fragrance.

• 建兰
Cymbidium Ensifolium

春兰，别名"草兰""山兰"，分布较广，尤以江苏、福建、广东、四川、云南、江西、甘肃、台湾等地为多。花期为每年2—3月，花开时间可持续一个月之久。花朵颜色有红色、绿色、黄绿色等，通常在萼片及花瓣上有紫褐色

Cymbidium goeringii (*Chunlan*, literally spring orchid), also known as grass orchid or mountain orchid, is widely distributed especially in provinces like Jiangsu, Fujian, Guangdong, Sichuan, Yunnan, Jiangxi, Gansu and Taiwan. The flowering lasts for one month from February to March. The aromatic blossom can vary from red, green to yellow-green in color, with purple-brown stripes or speckles on the sepals and petals. Among all others, Cymbidium goeringii has the largest distribution in China and a long history of cultivation and therefore is most commonly seen. Besides, in terms of floral shapes, it can be further divided into six categories, i.e. lotus-petaled, plum-blossom-petaled, narcissus-petaled, oddly petaled, commonly petaled as well as multi-petaled cultivars.

Cymbidium faberi (*Huilan*), also known as *Jiujie* Orchid, or Summer Orchid, is the oldest type of Chinese orchid with the longest cultivation history. Many fine varieties are selected from wild orchid that are noted for their cold resistance and widely distributed in the northernmost China. It usually flowers from March to May. The root is thick and long. The leaves are narrow and band-shaped, verdant in color, rough and

• 墨兰
Cymbidium Sinense

的条纹或斑块，气味芳香浓郁。春兰是中国兰花中分布最广、最常见且栽培历史悠久的一种，以花形不同，又可分为荷瓣型、梅瓣型、水仙瓣型、奇瓣型、普通化型和多花型六大类。

hard in texture with prominent midribs. The blossom have enduring fragrance and a rich color, and the commonest is light yellow. In the Chinese tradition, people distinguished those with one flower on one stalk from those with many, and the former are known as *Lan*, whereas the latter are called *Hui*. Huang Tingjian, a famous poet in the Northern Song Dynasty also saw the difference between these two orchid and specifically highlighted *Lan* for its lingering fragrance. This can be regarded as the initial standard adopted to distinguish the one from the other.

Cymbidium ensifolium (*Jianlan*) is named after its place of origin Fujian Province, also known as Robust Orchid, River *Jun* Orchid, Summer *Hui*, etc. This type of cymbidium is sturdy and upright with verdant leaves, elegant flowers and a rich fragrance. It can withstand both summer heat and wintry cold, is full of vitality and easy to cultivate. Different kinds of cymbidium ensifolium can vary in flowering phase, most of them bloom from July to December, but some can flower from May to December. Thus it is also known as Cymbidium of the Four Seasons.

Cymbidium kankan (*Hanlan*,

蕙兰，又叫"九节兰""夏兰"，是中国兰花中栽培历史最古老的种类之一，并从野生植株中发展出了许多优良品种，同时它是在中国分布最北的兰花品种，耐寒能力较强。蕙兰花期在3—5月，根部粗而长，叶为狭带形，苍绿色，质地粗糙、坚硬，中脉显著。花朵浓香持久，色彩丰富，以浅黄色最常见。中国传统上对一茎一花的兰花称"兰"，一茎多花的称"蕙"，以示区别。北宋诗人黄庭坚称："一干一花而香有余者，兰；一干数花而香不足者，蕙。"这可以说是区别兰和蕙的最初标准。

建兰，因原产于中国福建地区而得名，又名"雄兰""骏河兰""夏蕙"等。建兰健壮挺拔，叶子青翠欲滴，花朵芳香馥郁，不惧暑，不畏寒，生命力强，容易栽培。不同品种的建兰花期各异，大部分在7—10月，有些类型从5—12月均可开花，故又名"四季兰"。

寒兰，主要分布在福建、浙江、江西、湖南、广东等地，花期多在10—12月，因而得名。寒兰的叶片比建兰更为细长，叶片基部更

literally cold orchid) mainly grows in Fujian, Zhejiang, Jiangxi, Hunan and Guangdong provinces. As cymbidium kankan mostly flowers in winter from October to December, it thus gets its name. Its leaves are slenderer than those of the cymbidium ensifolium, the base of its blade is also thinner, and moreover cymbidium kankan usually assumes a fine elegance tinged with comely verdure. The flower is slender in form, bright and fresh in color, emitting a well-proportioned grace and a vibrant hue.

• 寒兰
Cymbidium Kankan

细，姿态幽雅潇洒，碧绿清秀。花形瘦而长，花色艳丽、鲜美，显得匀称飘逸，充满生机。

墨兰，又叫"报岁兰"，原产于广东、广西、福建、台湾、云南等地。墨兰叶片硕大而亮丽，姿态飘逸，四季常青，有"看叶胜看花"之誉。开花时花朵呈淡褐色，色彩淡雅，幽香四溢，再加上花期一般在2月，正值春节期

Cymbidium sinense (*MoLan*), also known as *Baosui* Orchid (literally orchid heralding the Spring Festival), is native to provinces and regions like Guangdong, Guangxi, Fujian, Taiwan and Yunnan. The leaves are huge, radiant, graceful and moreover evergreen, hence are cherished more than the flowers. The pale brown flowers are quite elegant in color with sweet aroma overflowing. As the cymbidium sinense often comes to bloom in February precisely during the Spring Festival, it is also named *Baosui* Orchid and therefore finds great favor with the Chinese.

Since the aroma of orchid is mild, pure and profound, it has long been held as the very essence of Chinese cymbidium. The ancients often used

- 京剧大师梅兰芳在《贵妃醉酒》中的"兰花指"

传统戏曲表演中，女子手势多做"兰花指"，模仿兰花花朵的形状，可见兰花的姿态美深受人们喜爱。

Orchid-shaped Finger Gesture by Mei Lanfang, the Great Master of Peking Opera in the *Drunken Beauty*

In traditional opera performances, women often use their fingers to mimic the shape of the orchid, called orchid-shaped finger, from which we can see how people adore the orchid for its graceful gesture.

间，所以得名"报岁兰"，深得人们的喜爱。

　　兰花的香气温和、纯正、深远，自古被看作中国兰花的精髓，古人曾用"国香""王者之香""天下第一香"来形容它。赏兰的人都有"一盆在室，满屋皆香"的体验，这种幽香时有时无，时浓时淡，时远时近，给人们带来清新而愉悦的感受。这种带点神秘感的幽香，是其他花卉的香气无法比拟的。兰香历来被当作评估鉴定兰花的重要标准，一般以清香浓郁而持久者为上品。若以香气的浓淡程度比较，春兰最浓郁，建兰第二，寒兰次之，接下来是墨兰和蕙兰。

national fragrance, the king of all fragrances or the No. 1 fragrance under heaven to describe its eminence. For orchid appreciation, most people would have a potted one in their room to relish its aroma, which only bursts occasionally, now rich now faint, now far now near, yet fresh and pleasant. No other floral aroma can be compared with such mysterious scent. Hence all through the ages, fragrance has been regarded as an important criterion to evaluate an orchid. Generally it holds those of rich and enduring fragrance as the top grade. And in light of the fragrant density, the cymbidium goeringii is most aromatic, cymbidium ensifolium takes the second place, cymbidium kankan follows it, and finally come the cymbidium sinense and cymbidium faberi.

王羲之与兰亭

兰亭，在浙江绍兴西南的兰渚山下。古籍《越绝书》中提到，春秋时期越王勾践曾经在渚山种植兰花，所以后人也称渚山为"兰渚山"。相传汉朝时此地有过驻亭，所以后来便有了"兰亭"的雅称。兰花喜阴，常生长在靠近水源的地方，"兰亭"便坐落在这样一个极适宜兰花生长的地方。东晋时期的大书法家王羲之曾作《兰亭集序》，记述了他和朋友们来到兰亭修禊祈福的事情。暮春三月，出类拔萃的才俊名流都聚集在此地，其中既有年少的孩子，也有年长的老者，场面很是热闹。四周有高大、险峻的山峰环抱，树木繁茂，更有挺拔秀丽的竹林参差掩映，河水清澈见底。大家按顺序列坐在曲折的河流两边，一边欣赏自然美景，一边饮酒吟诗，其乐融融。

Wang Xizhi and Orchid Pavilion

The Orchid Pavilion is located at the foot of Lanzhu Mountain southwest of Shaoxing City, Zhejiang Province. According to the ancient book *Lost History of Yue*, Gou Jian, the King of State Yue during the Spring and Autumn Period (770 B.C.-476 B.C.), once planted orchid (*Lan* in Chinese) in Zhu Mountain, so future generations also call it Lanzhu Mountain. Another legend has that in the Han Dynasty (206 B.C.-220 A.D.), a pavilion was built there and thus the poetic appellation Orchid Pavilion came into being. Orchid prefers to grow in a shaded area by water, and the Orchid Pavilion is exactly located in such a place. Wang Xizhi, the noted calligrapher of the Eastern Jin Dynasty once wrote the famous *Preface to the Poems Composed at the Orchid Pavilion* here, which describes a gathering with friends at the Orchid Pavilion for the Spring Purification Festival. In late spring, all remarkable scholars and celebrities would gather here, old and young, making a lively spectacle. Lofty mountains, luxuriant trees and handsome bamboos embrace the pavilion; a limpid stream gurgles around. People took seat orderly on both sides of the river. They enjoyed the natural beauty, sharing wine from floating goblet while chanting poems. The air was filled with joy.

• 王羲之像
Portrait of Wang Xizhi

- 浙江绍兴兰亭"鹅池"碑亭

  绍兴兰亭的三角形碑亭中立着刻有"鹅池"二字的石碑，传说"鹅池"两字为王羲之的手笔。

Goose Pond Pavilion with Stone-stele at Shaoxing City, Zhejiang Province

In the triangle tablet pavilion of the Orchid Pavilion, there is the famous goose pond stone stele carved with two Chinese characters *E Chi*, literally goose pond. It is said that the two characters were written by Wang Xizhi.

- 流觞曲水

  流觞曲水，最初是中国古人每年农历三月三日在水边进行的祈福活动，后来逐渐发展成为文人临水赋诗、饮酒赏景的风雅之举。"觞"是古代盛酒器，类似酒杯，通常为木制，小而体轻，底部有托，可浮于水中。大家坐在水渠两旁，在上游放置觞，任其顺流而下，停在谁的面前，谁就得即兴赋诗并饮酒。

Winding Streamlet Where the Goblets Float

Having the goblets float on the winding streamlet was originally a yearly ritual performed waterside by the ancient Chinese to pray for blessings on the third day of the third month of the lunar calendar. Later however, it became a refined activity particular to literati who would chant, drink and enjoy the scenery by the river. Goblet is an ancient drinking vessel similar to our wine glass, but wooden, small and light, with a flat bottom so that it can float on water. Usually people would sit on both sides of the stream, place the goblet in the upper reaches and let it flow down with the current. The person before whom it stops is expected to drink and improvise a poem.

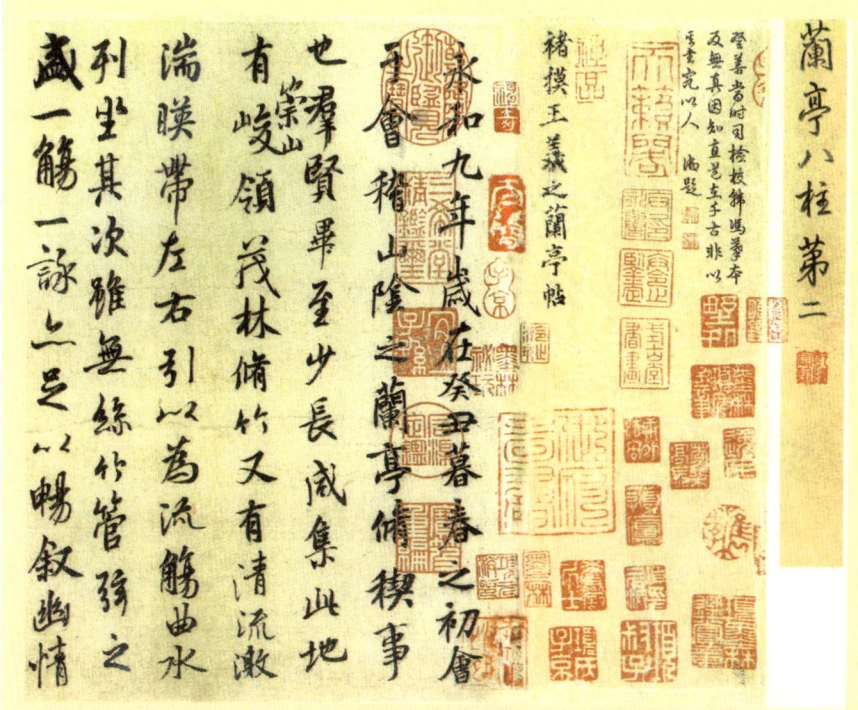

- **褚遂良临摹王羲之《兰亭集序》【局部】（唐）**

  王羲之在精研书法体势时，更得益于爱兰。兰叶青翠欲滴、素静整洁、疏密相宜、流畅飘逸。王羲之将兰叶的各种姿态运用到书法中，使他的书法结构、笔法、章法的技巧达到精熟的高度。他的书法字体秀美，错落自然，达到了神韵生动、随心所欲的境界。《兰亭集序》全文书法遒劲飘逸，是王羲之的得意之作，被历代书家推为"天下第一行书"。唐初，酷爱王羲之书法的唐太宗李世民在得到《兰亭集序》真迹后，曾命当朝书法名家褚遂良等人摹写数本，流传至今。

  Copy of Wang Xizhi's *Preface to the Poems Composed at the Orchid Pavilion* by Chu Suiliang [Partial] (Tang Dynasty, 618-907)

  Wang Xizhi benefited a lot from his affinity for orchid when studying calligraphic structure. The orchid leaves outshine with a fresh verdure, a simple air of neatness, a balanced density, and a smooth elegance. Wang Xizhi skillfully applied the various postures of the orchid into calligraphy, as a result of which he achieved mastery in calligraphic structure, strokes and techniques. His calligraphy is not only comely in style, but naturally scattered with a vivid charm and freewheeling verve. *Preface to the Poems Composed at the Orchid Pavilion* was written in vigorous yet elegant brushstrokes. It is Wang Xizhi's finest creation and also greeted as No. 1 Running Script under Heaven by calligraphers of all ages. In the early Tang Dynasty, Emperor Taizong, Li Shimin, loved Wang Xizhi's calligraphy so much that when he got the authentic manuscript of *Preface*, he immediately ordered Chu Suiliang and other famous calligraphers of the times to make copies, which survive to the very present.

> 兰之品格

人们欣赏兰花的芳香，兰叶的优美，兰开花时，幽香清远；无花时，优雅常青的叶片参差交错，随风摇曳，婀娜多姿，古人对兰花曾有"观叶胜观花"的赞叹。而兰花最让人倾心之处就在于它的"幽洁"，虽生长在深山野谷、悬崖绝壁，却能彰显出本性之美。古人认为兰花具有"人不知而不愠"的风度，不求闻达、自乐其志的坦荡胸襟，最符合中国人谦冲自持的人格观。历代高人隐士总习惯在兰花的幽洁中寄寓自身坚贞高洁的精神品性。

兰花的香气清雅幽远，古来有"王者香"的美誉。远在2000多年前的春秋时代，儒家学说创始人、大思想家孔子由卫国返回鲁国，中

> Noble Character of Orchid

People appreciate the fragrance of orchid and its delicate leaves. When it blooms, the aroma flows far away; when it is flowerless, the evergreen leaves alone shine forth. They interlace with one another, swaying in the wind so gracefully that it is no wonder that the ancients would marvel at the leaves rather than the flowers. The most enchanting part of an orchid lies in its serenity. Though growing in the deep mountain valley by sheer cliff, it manifests no less beauty of nature. The ancients believed that orchid has a lofty demeanor and a magnanimous mind which does not seek fame but follow its own pursuit. Such a character mostly agrees with the modest and self-restrained personality advocated by Chinese. High-minded scholars and hermits of all generations would resort to the serene orchid and find

途经过隐谷，突然闻到阵阵清香。孔子循香寻去，发现山谷中的草丛里盛开着一大片兰花。孔子当场叹道："夫兰为王者香，今乃独茂，与众草为伍，譬犹贤者不逢时，与鄙夫为伦也。"大意是：兰本应是王者所佩的香草，而今却在这幽谷中独自繁茂，与杂草为伍，就好比贤良的人生不逢时，却和粗鄙的人一起被埋没了。孔子不但欣赏兰的

spiritual sustenance in its faithful and noble character.

The aroma of orchid is soft and far-reaching. Since the ancient times, it has been honored as King of All Fragrances. About 2000 years ago in the Spring and Autumn Period (770 B.C.-476 B.C.), Confucius the great thinker and also founder of Confucianism returned to the State of Lu from the State of Wei together with his followers. When they passed the Hidden Valley, suddenly a lovely smell burst out. Confucius pursued its source and found a large number of orchid blooming in the grass. He exclaimed on the spot, "Orchid should be used to adorn the noble, but now it thrives alone in the dell, mixed with the weeds. It is like a virtuous person born at the wrong time, thus buried together with the vulgar." Confucius not only enjoyed the beauty

- 《孔子像》马远（宋）

孔子曾说过："与善人居，如入芝兰之室，久而不闻其香，即与之化矣。"意思是：和品行优良的人交往，就好像进入了摆满兰花的芳香的房间，久而久之闻不到兰花的香味了，这是因为自己和香味融为一体了。

Portrait of Confucius, by Ma Yuan (Song Dynasty, 960-1279)

As Confucius once observed, when you associate with the virtuous people, it feels like entering a room filled with fragrant orchid; over time you will not smell the aroma, because you have been soaked in it.

• 《溪山兰若图》【局部】巨然（宋）
Orchid with Streams and Mountains by Juran [Partial] (Song Dynasty, 960-1279)

美与芳，更佩服兰的志与节，他还曾说："芝兰生于深林，不以无人而不芳。君子修道立德，不谓穷困而改节。"将兰花比喻为君子，孔子是第一人。

and fragrance of orchid, but spoke highly of its integrity. Indeed he is the first who compared orchid to a gentleman. He said, "Born in the forest, orchid will not hide its perfume because no one appreciates it; this just resembles the self-cultivation

战国时期的诗人屈原是楚国的大臣，他曾因直言进谏而遭到猜忌，被放逐。屈原在流放的途中，忧国忧民，写下了浪漫主义的不朽诗篇《离骚》。诗中歌颂了兰花之

of a gentleman who will not desert principles even in destitute."

The poet Qu Yuan was a minister in the State of Chu during the Warring States Period (475 B.C.-221 B.C.). Once he was banished for his plain speaking in

• 《屈子行吟图》傅抱石（现代）
Qu Yuan Singing and Strolling, by Fu Baoshi (Modern Times)

美，把它视为崇高与圣洁的象征。屈原在故乡秭归时，曾在庭院、田园种满了兰花。他还经常佩戴兰花，以示自己洁身自好、不与小人同流合污。他还愤怒地抨击了那些使兰失去芳香，进而变若茅草的小人。他一生爱兰、颂兰，将兰作为一种寄托、一种象征，一种精神与品格的追求。可以说，屈原用他流传千古的伟大诗作，奠定了中国兰文化的根基。

兰花的品格得到人们的喜爱，兰花也逐渐从山野移居到人们的家中。古人把养兰花称为"艺兰"，人们养兰、观兰、闻兰，与兰花朝夕相处，正是为陶冶性情，学习兰花高洁的品格。

宋代文学家黄庭坚曾经在四川戎州（今四川宜宾）做过地方官。戎州附近有一座山叫"兰山"，山中有野生兰花。黄庭坚将之移栽于庭院中，并建起一座亭子，命名为"幽芳亭"。黄庭坚在《书幽芳亭》一文中写道："兰甚似乎君子，生于深山薄丛之中，不为无人而不芳；雪霜凌厉而见杀，来岁不改其性也。是所谓'遁世无闷，不见是而无闷'者也。"意思是：兰

the court. In exile he was still concerned about the fate of the nation, and thus wrote *Lisao,* an immortal piece of romanticism. In the poem, he extolled the beauty of orchid, regarding it as a symbol of nobility and holiness. In fact, he planted orchid at the courtyard and garden in his hometown Zigui. Besides, he often wore it to show his righteousness never in cahoots with the villain, and even fiercely

- 屈原像
Portrait of Qu Yuan

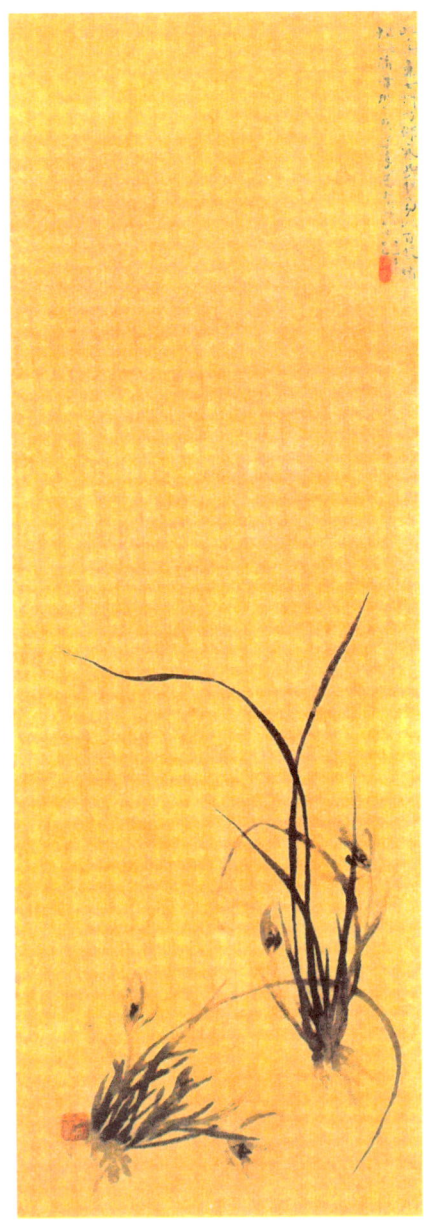

《兰花图》石涛（清）

The Orchid, by Shi Tao (Qing Dynasty, 1616-1911)

criticized those who deprived the orchid of its aroma and hence reduced it into plain thatch. He devoted the whole life to the beloved orchid, sang highly of it, reposed in it for spiritual sustenance, and pursued it for its noble character. As it were, by this classic poem, Qu Yuan laid the foundation of Chinese orchid culture.

Cherished for its noble character, orchid gradually moved from the wilderness to the household. In the ancient times, the orchid cultivation was known as an art. People plant, appreciate and smell it all day long, they closely associate with it just to cultivate their own mind and learn from it the virtue of a very gentleman.

Huang Tingjian, the great man of letters in the Northern Song Dynasty once served as a local official in Rongzhou (now Yibin City), Sichuan Province. Nearby was an Orchid Mountain where wild orchid grew in wanton profusion. For individual delight, Huang Tingjian transplanted them in his own courtyard and also built an Aromatic Pavilion named after their fragrance. In his *Prose on the Aromatic Pavilion*, he remarked that orchid strongly resembles the gentleman in character. It grows in the deep forested mountains, letting out

花的品格非常像君子，虽然生长在深山老林之中，却不因为无人赏识而不芳香。在遭受雪霜残酷的摧残后，也不改变自己的本性。这正是《易经》中说的隐居却不烦闷的境界，就像君子修身养性、自得其乐，虽然得不到世人的赞同也并不烦恼。

fragrance even if no one appreciates it and will not change nature despite the fierce attack of savage weather. This is exactly the state of mind highlighted in the *Book of Changes*, which is at once far from the madding crowd, just like that of a gentleman who rejoices in self-cultivation with no worry about worldly approbation.

- 翡翠兰花盆景
Emerald Orchid Bonsai

> ## 墨兰清雅

以兰花比德于君子的传统，在中国古代诗文和书画的创作上也有很好的体现。唐代大诗人卢纶有"佳人比香草，君子即芳兰"之句。唐太宗李世民认为只有君子才配得上折兰以佩。兰花代表君子，成为一种品德的象征，其他的那些荆棘之类的杂草便被作为君子的对立面，有了"小人"的寓意。因此，传统兰竹绘画作品中经常可以见到丛兰之中生有荆棘，之所以这

> ## Refined Elegance of Ink Orchid

The tradition to use orchid as symbol of a gentleman's virtue is well represented in the creation of ancient Chinese poetry, prose, painting and calligraphy. Lu Lun, a great poet of the Tang Dynasty once compared a beauty to sweet vanilla and a gentleman to fragrant orchid. Emperor Taizong of the Tang Dynasty, Li Shimin believed that only a gentleman deserved orchid as ornament. Thus orchid symbolizes the moral integrity of gentlemen, while other thorny weeds

样画，一是为了交代兰花生长的环境，更重要的是比喻君子能包容小人的高贵品质。有些画家在创作写意兰花时，特意把兰花的根一并画出来，盘根郁结，宛如乱麻纠缠，偏偏有着一种顽强的生命力。

are regarded as the very opposite with the implication of villains. Therefore, in traditional orchid or bamboo paintings, we can often see brambles among the orchid. In this way artists not only account for the living environment of orchid, but

- 《漪兰竹石图》【局部】文徵明（明）

明代画家文徵明一生爱兰、画兰，他笔下的兰花飘逸潇洒，有"文兰"之誉。这幅《漪兰竹石图》，可以说是他画兰的代表作。在1.2米的长卷中，展现出一道松荫清溪、兰蕙竞芳的幽谷，三十多丛兰蕙散生在怪石、崖坡之间，或上或下，或前或后，或隐或现，或正或侧，或直立，或倒挂，无不各得其宜，窈窕有致，既有条理又浑然天成，再加上翠竹野草的衬托，更使画面生动自然。兰叶之中处处显现出书法笔意，极具动感之美。

Riverside Orchid, Bamboo and Rock [Partial] by Wen Zhengming (Ming Dynasty, 1368-1644)

Wen Zhengming (1470-1559), the noted Chinese painter in the Ming Dynasty was fond of orchid and also liked painting it. His orchid is known for its refined elegance and this painting can well represent his remarkable achievement. As the 1.2 meters (3.9 ft) long scroll unfolds, we see shady pines by a limpid stream and a dell where *Lan* and *Hui* (two kinds of orchid) compete in fragrance. More than thirty clusters of cymbidium scatter between the grotesque rocks and the cliff, above or below, on the front or at the back, partly hidden, partly visible. Some face us, some turn sideways; some stand upright, some hang upside down; all show their best with trim and natural elegance. The verdant bamboo and weeds further set off their lissome figure, rendering the whole picture more vivid. From the orchid leaves we can also trace the influence of Chinese calligraphy which grants the flowers a dynamic beauty.

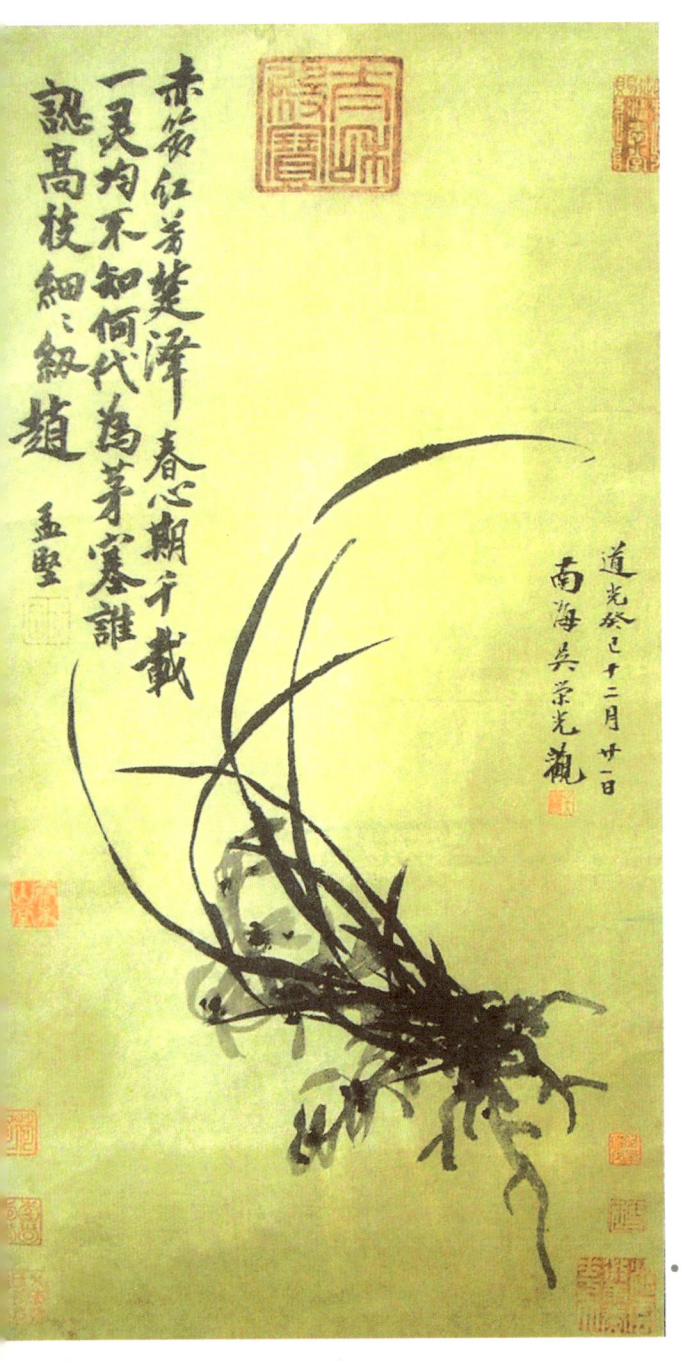

moreover enhance the noble quality of a gentleman who is magnanimous enough to accommodate villains. When creating orchid in freehand brushwork, some painters would deliberately illuminate every root of the flower, intertwined and entangled like a mess but with strong vitality.

Zhao Mengjian, a prestigious artist in the late Southern Song Dynasty was especially good at painting orchid. *Cymbidium Goeringii Scroll* now collected in the Palace Museum is one of his masterpieces. Zhao Mengjian came from the imperial clan and was the 11th generation descendent of the Emperor Taizu (the founder of the Song Dynasty). He is a typical Confucian scholar. Of royal blood, he desired to make contributions. Zhao Mengjian retired to Haiyan County in Zhejiang Province with his families. Later generations adored his talent and pride. Besides, different from orchid painters of former generations,

《墨兰图》赵孟坚（南宋）
Ink Orchid, by Zhao Mengjian (Southern Song Dynasty, 1127-1279)

- 《墨兰图》赵孟坚（南宋）

赵孟坚所画的兰花花疏叶简，笔力劲健，兰根暴露，意趣纵横。

Ink Orchid, by Zhao Mengjian (Souther Song Dynasty, 1127-1279)

Zhao Mengjian's orchid usually have sparse and simple leaves and exposed roots. By vigorous brushwork the painting appeals with natural interest.

　　宋末颇负盛名的画家赵孟坚是一位画兰高手，现藏于故宫博物院的《春兰画卷》便是他的代表作。赵孟坚是南宋宗室，宋太祖的十一世孙。他是一名典型的儒士，作为宋室后裔的他渴望建功立业、施展抱负，后携家眷隐居在浙江海盐。后人倾慕他的才华与傲骨。与前代画兰名家不同的是，赵孟坚画兰不画土，称为"露根兰"。他将精力倾注于所创作的墨兰之中，使得他笔下的兰花也拥有了独特的气息。

　　清代画家金农在画作上的题诗中，曾提到一位女画家"金陵马四

Zhao Mengjian usually paints orchid as soilless with exposed root. He put his energy into all his creations, and also given his ink orchid a unique air.

　　Jin Nong, a Chinese painter in the Qing Dynasty once mentioned a female painter in one of his poetic inscriptions "Ma Siniang in Jinling", that is Ma Shouzhen, in the Ming Dynasty in Nanjing, Jiangsu Province. Ma Shouzhen, also known as Ma Xianglan, is usually called Siniang (literally the fourth lady), for she was the fourth child of the family. According to the legend, she was broad-minded and righteous. She desired in heart to be as noble as orchid. She not only planted orchid in the courtyard, but was fond of painting it, and often compared herself to orchid in poems, then indulged in self-admiration. As she was born in southern Hunan Province (*Xiang* for short), and also very fond of orchid (*Lan* in Chinese), she often inscribed the name Xianglan on the paintings. Her two volumes of poetry are also named *Collection of Xianglan*, and hence people began to call her by this literary name.

Ma Shouzhen was expert in poetry and painting and particularly good at painting orchid. With natural grace and rustic charm, the orchid in her works shares a lot of similarities with the flowers created by male literati painters, especially the painters of Wumen School like Wen Zhengming. Her works sold quite well and soon became famous. Indeed her fans with painted orchid even found market overseas.

- 《芝兰图》马守真（明）

Ganoderma and Orchid, by Ma Shouzhen (Ming Dynasty, 1368-1644)

娘",即明朝时的马守真。马守真（1548—1604），也叫马湘兰，因在家中排行第四，人称"四娘"。相传她为人旷达，颇有豪侠之气。马守真内心渴望做个像兰花一样高洁的女子。她不仅在庭院中大量种植兰花，而且还酷爱画兰，常在诗中将自己比作兰花，孤芳自赏。因她祖籍湖南（简称"湘"），又酷爱兰花，常在画幅中题名"湘兰子"，所写的两卷诗集也命名为《湘兰集》，人们也就以"湘兰"来称呼她。

马守真能诗善画，尤擅画兰，她笔下的兰花具有脱俗的飘逸之气与野趣，与男性文人画家，尤其是"吴门画派"中文徵明等人的兰花有着许多相近之处。她的作品因时人竞相购存而名扬天下，画兰扇面等甚至漂洋过海远销到国外。

Zheng Banqiao, a distinguished painter and calligrapher in the Qing Dynasty was also good at painting orchid. He often compared himself to orchid and regarded it as Incense of the

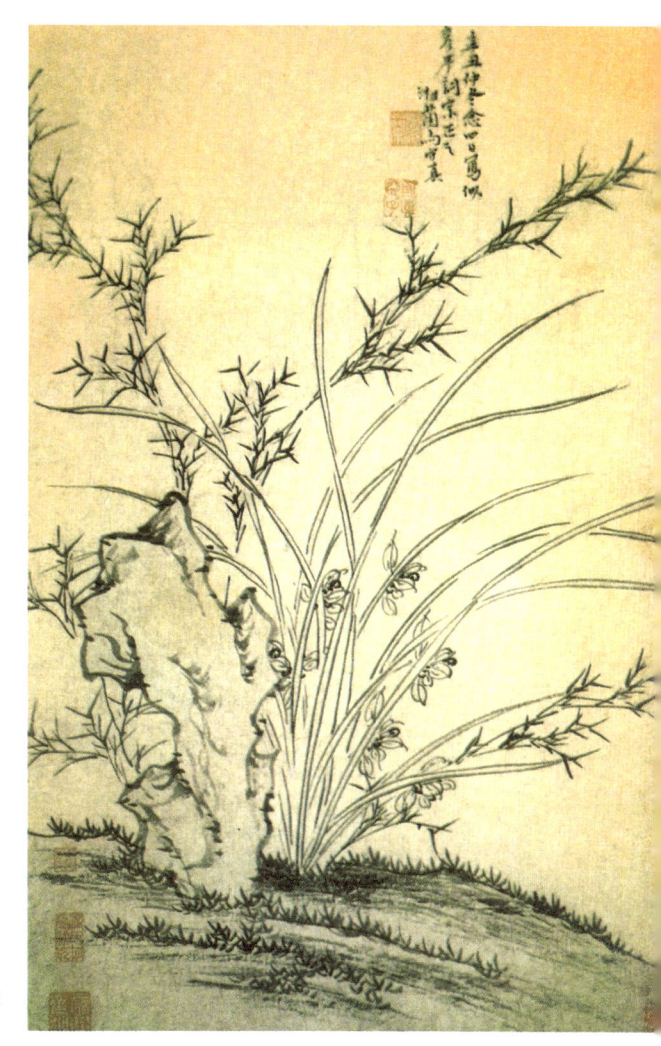

- 《兰竹图》马守真（明）
  Orchid and Bamboo, by Ma Shouzhen (Ming Dynasty, 1368-1644)

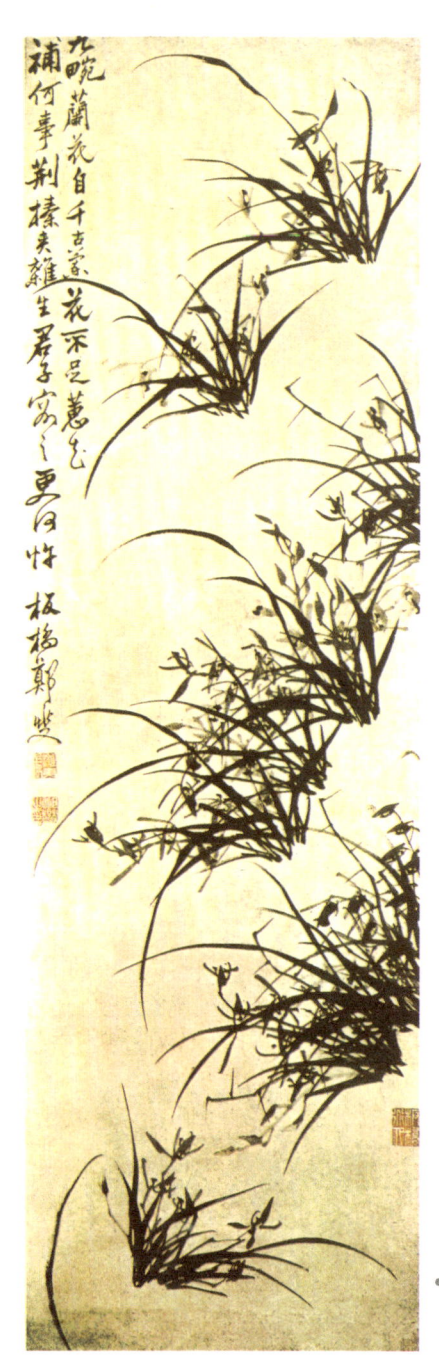

Zheng Household. He loved, praised and portrayed orchid largely because of the impact from Qu Yuan. He borrowed lines from *Lisao* to embellish his orchid paintings and convey his longings, claiming that his orchid retains the noble character of Qu Yuan. As the story goes, once Zheng Banqiao noticed a potted orchid in his residence pined away in listless gesture, so he broke the pot immediately and transplanted the orchid in the courtyard. In early spring of the next year, this orchid flourished just as expected. Overcome with emotion, Zheng Banqiao wrote a poem on the spot, saying that, "Orchid is originally a mountain plant, so it should grow in its native place; many people try to cultivate it in pots, but it is better to leave it with the rosy clouds."

Among all ancient orchid painters, some are good at representing its posture, some underline its nature, Zheng Banqiao, however, paid equal attention

- 《兰草图》郑板桥（清）

Orchid, by Zheng Banqiao (Qing Dynasty, 1616-1911)

清代书画家郑板桥擅长画兰,常以兰花自喻,把兰花称为"郑家香"。他之所以爱兰、咏兰、写兰,在很大程度上是受了屈原的影响,他借《离骚》之句画兰寄情,称所画之兰为"屈大夫之清风"。据说有一回,郑板桥留意到家中盆养的兰花姿态憔悴,无精打采,便捣碎花盆,将兰花移栽在庭院前。来年初春,这株兰花果然长势喜人。郑板桥在感慨之余,挥笔题诗道:

兰花本是山中草,还向山中种此花。
尘世纷纷植盆盎,不如留与伴烟霞。

古人画兰,有人善于表现兰的姿态,有人重于表现兰的本质,而郑板桥则是姿态、本质并重,而题跋往往突出一个"香"字。郑板桥 to both and tended to highlight the orchid fragrance almost in all his inscriptions. Zheng Banqiao's orchid mostly grows in the mountains. By heavy ink and a cursive style, he fully brought out the romantic nature of the flower in its

- 《幽兰图》郑板桥(清)

  寥寥几笔水墨的叶,叶间映出淡淡的花,静静地依在画面的一角。再衬上几行洒落的字、一方小小红印,书香气自然扑鼻而来。

  Ink Orchid, by Zheng Banqiao (Qing Dynasty, 1616-1911)

  Some light-colored flowers emerge among a few leaves by ink and wash, and quietly repose in one corner of the painting. Several lines of running script, together with a tiny red seal mark, let out a literary aroma that salutes our nostrils.

所画的兰花，大多是山野之兰，他以重墨草书之笔尽情挥洒出兰花的浪漫天性，侧重表现兰花的秀雅多姿。清代的杨复明对郑板桥的兰画有这样的评价："画兰之法，贵秀逸而非柔媚，贵奔放而非粗野，贵峭健而非生硬，贵朴茂而非拙塞。"

refined elegance. Yang Fuming, a scholar in the Qing Dynasty once remarked on Zheng Banqiao's orchid paintings, saying that orchid should be painted as elegant rather than coquettish, bold rather than rough, vigorous rather than stiff, simple and honest rather than clumsy and crowded.

兰桂齐芳

"兰桂齐芳"是中国传统的吉祥图案，由兰花与桂花组成。兰花姿态优美，品性高洁，因此古人常以佩兰喻品德高尚之人。而桂花树也是崇高、贞洁、荣誉、友好和吉祥的象征，古人常将桂花当作礼物送人，用"折桂"来比喻学子考中科举。所以"兰桂齐芳"寓意家运兴隆，子孙品行高洁，个个成才，荣华富贵。

Orchid and Osmanthus in Bloom

It is a traditional auspicious design in China made up of orchid and osmanthus. For its graceful gesture and noble character, the ancients often use orchid as symbol of one's moral integrity. The osmanthus tree is also an emblem of eminence, chastity, honor, friendship and good fortune, so the ancient Chinese usually give the sweet-scented osmanthus as a present, or pluck a branch of the tree to laurel those who passed the imperial examination. Therefore this idiom "Orchid and Osmanthus in Bloom" implies prosperity of the family and virtue of the descendants who all achieve success to be rich and famous.

- 《兰桂齐芳》扇面（近代）
Painted Fan of *Orchid and Osmanthus in Bloom* (Modern Times)

说竹
Ode to the Bamboo

  竹子四季青翠，挺拔坚劲，而又空心、有节。中国古人认为，君子就应该像竹子一样坚定，要虚怀若谷，守节坚贞。

  竹，属于多年生禾本科植物，有木质化的或长或短的地下茎。竿为木质化，有明显的节，节间中空。竹子的幼芽叫作竹笋，历来作为鲜美的蔬菜食用。

Bamboo is evergreen in four seasons, upright with joints and hollow inside. In the Chinese belief, one should be just as firm as the bamboo, so as to be righteous, impartial, open-minded and faithful throughout.

  Bamboo is a perennial gramineous plant with lignified long or short underground stems. The woody stem is jointed and hollow inside. The new buds are referred to as bamboo shoots, which have served a wonderful dish since the ancient times.

> 竹之品赏

竹适合生长的地域非常广，在中国的大江南北均能看到竹子，它主要分布于长江流域及华南、西南等地。中国的竹子种类很丰富，大约有300种之多。南方以毛竹最为常见，又名"江南竹"，这种竹子的生长速度特别快，大约一个半月的时间就能长到二十来米。

大多数竹子的竿、枝、叶都是翠绿的，而且一年四季都是如此，被古人称为"碧琅玕"，而今天人们喜欢用"翠竹"来指称竹子。其实，竹子的颜色也是丰富多彩的。比如有一种碧玉嵌黄金竹，翠绿如碧玉，但节间的沟槽为金黄色的纵条纹；还有一种黄金间碧玉竹与前者正相反，色泽金黄，节间却有宽窄不等的绿色纵条纹。

> Appreciation of Bamboo

Bamboo is adaptable to most geographical area from north to south over China, but mainly distributed in the Yangtze River valley, South China, and the Southwest, etc. China is really rich with more than 300 species of bamboo, among which the Mao bamboo (of the genus phyllostachys), also known as bamboo south of the Yangtze River, is most common in the South. This kind of bamboo grows very fast. In about one and a half months, it will be over 20 meters (65.6 ft) tall.

Most bamboos have evergreen pole, branch and leaves, hence known among the ancients as Jasper-Like Plant and even nowadays people like referring to it as green bamboo. Actually bamboo is also rich in color. For instance, there is a kind of bamboo in green as jasper yet embedded with golden stripes between

• 黄金嵌碧玉竹
Green bamboo with golden stripes

除了竹竿上有不同颜色的条纹外，还有点缀有不同颜色和斑点的竹子，最典型的当数斑竹。斑竹生长在湖南九嶷山中，竹竿上有紫褐色或淡褐色的斑点，犹如血泪凝固而成，故又称"泪竹"。由于有湘妃的传说，故又称"湘妃竹"。

紫竹又名"黑竹""竹茄"，新长成的幼竹本是翠绿色，一年以后，逐渐出现紫斑，最后全部变为紫黑色，色泽柔和发亮，隐于绿叶之下，十分绮丽。古人常将紫竹种植于庭院山石之间，或植于书斋、

the joints, whereas another variety is just the reverse, with golden color and green vertical stripes varied in width.

In addition to those with colorful stripes on the pole, there are also bamboos dotted with different colors and speckles, among which the mottled bamboo is most typical. It is a phyllostachys bamboo species native in Jiuyi Mountain, Hunan Province. There are purple-brown or light-brown spots on the pole solidified as if by tear drops, so people also refer to it as Tear Bamboo. Besides, it is also known as Xiangfei Bamboo due to the legend of Xiangfei.

Purple bamboo is also known as black bamboo or bamboo eggplant. A young bamboo is usually emerald green; about one year later, purple spots begin to emerge and soon cover it all with purplish black which radiates a soft luster under the green leaves. Considering its high ornamental value, the ancients often planted the black bamboo between the rockwork in the garden, in the study or hall, on the path, or by the pond. Besides, this kind of bamboo usually features a tough pole which can be made into fishing rod, walking stick or instruments like bamboo flute, horizontal or vertical.

Sasa fortunei (or dwarf white-stripe bamboo) is about 25 cm (about 9.84 inches) tall. This little bamboo is particularly characterized by vertical white or pale yellow stripes and white

- 紫竹
Purple Bamboo

厅堂、小径、池水旁，具有很高的观赏价值。同时，紫竹的竹竿较为坚韧，适宜做鱼竿、手杖及箫、笛等乐器。

菲白竹是一种低矮的小竹，高25厘米左右，最特别的是竹叶叶面上有白色或淡黄色的纵条纹，两面还有白色的柔毛，"菲白竹"即由此得名。古人会在案头、茶几上摆放一盆端庄秀雅的菲白竹，别具雅趣。

- 菲白竹
Sasa Fortunei

竹子属多年生禾本科植物，但数十年才开一次花。千百年来，人们栽种竹子一般都采取育苗的方法，从竹林中选取竹苗挖出移植，之后就可以大量长竹鞭，并从竹鞭上长出竹笋。

竹林里每年都会长笋，竹笋长大便成为竹子。笋芽一旦破土而出，生长速度很快。大型竹种由竹笋出土到展枝发叶，长成大竹约需60天左右，

pubescence on both sides of the leaf, just as its name suggests. The ancients would place a potted sasa fortunei of unique elegance on the desk or the teapoy, which really caters for a refined taste.

Bamboo is a perennial gramineous plant and only flowers at intervals as long as decades. Through the ages, people usually cultivate bamboo with the method of growing seedling, that is, select bamboo seedling from the grove and

- 生长中的竹笋
Growing Bamboo Shoots

- 刚长高的幼竹
Young Bamboos

而一些中小型竹种仅需30天左右。竹子生长最快的时候日生长量可达1米左右，夜间生长尤其迅速。所以夜入竹林，有时可听到噼噼啪啪的响声，这是竹子拔节生长发出的声音。竹子不仅生长迅速，而且具有顽强的生命力。尤其是生长在黄河流域的竹子，要经受寒冷和干旱的考验。由于竹鞭入土较深，在地下形成一个密如蛛网的系统，因而比较耐寒和耐旱。一些扎根深山岩石中的竹子，能经受风吹雨打，坚

then transplant it, after which the bamboo rhizome will grow in large number and send out many shoots from its nodes.

Bamboo shoots spring up every year in the grove and gradually grow into a pole. Once the shoots emerge, they grow very quickly. The large bamboos usually come to full height in about 60 days, whereas some medium-and small-sized bamboos need only 30 days or less. The growth rate can reach one meter in 24 hours at best and is even higher at night. Indeed, when entering the bamboo grove at night, sometimes you can hear a crackling sound which is exactly made by the bamboo jointing. The bamboo is not only rapid in growth, but of strong vitality. Especially those in the Yellow River valley have to withstand the test of cold and drought. Since the rhizomes extend deep into the earth, they form a dense cobweb system under the ground and thus can tolerate varying climate or soil condition.

- **佛肚竹**

佛肚竹又称"罗汉竹""密节竹"，一般植株较矮，竹节较细，节间短而膨大。

Bambusa Ventricosa (or Buddha's Belly Bamboo)
Bambusa ventricosa, also known as Arhat bamboo or swollen-stemmed bamboo, is usually dwarf with thin joints and short yet swollen internodes.

苏州沧浪亭的竹间小径
Path Amidst Bamboo Grove by the Canglang Pavilion in Suzhou City

忍不拔，就是因为具有顽强的竹鞭系统。

竹子蕴含着丰富多样的美，自古以来为传统园林的造园艺人所应用，形成了一种中国特有的园艺美。早在夏商周时期，中国的先民就已懂得欣赏竹子的自然美。经过2000多年的不断实践，竹子已成为中国园林艺术的有机组成部分。江南园林的假山、石笋、水流旁常伴有竹子，廊轩亭榭之侧也常以修竹

Some persevering bamboos even root in the deep mountain rocks. They can endure the awful weather just because of their tenacious rhizome system.

Bamboo can be varied in beauty. Since ancient times, it has been employed in traditional gardening for its unique ornamental value. As early as in the Xia, Shang and Zhou dynasties, the ancient Chinese already began to appreciate bamboo's natural grace. After two thousand years of continuous practice, bamboo has become an integral part

• 《竹林品茗图》任伯年（清）
Painting of Enjoying Tea in Bamboo Grove, by Ren Bonian (Qing Dynasty, 1616-1911)

of Chinese gardening. For instance, in the gardens of regions soutn of the Yangtze River, you can see bamboo by the rockwork, stalagmite and riverside, or employed to adorn the corridor and pavilion. It brings about a contrasting effect of both softness and hardness,

• 扬州个园的竹丛

在用竹子造园方面，江苏省扬州市的个园堪称典范。个园，是一座以竹石斗奇而闻名的古典园林，园名"个"字就是对竹子形态的描摹。园内有竹60多种，数量过万株。置身于个园，放眼四望，到处蓬勃苍翠。

Bamboo Grove in the Geyuan Garden in Yangzhou City, Jiangsu Province

This classical garden is quite exemplary in the layout of bamboos and also famous for its unique design of bamboos and rocks. Indeed, we can trace the form of bamboo even in its Chinese name of the garden, *Ge* (个). There grow over ten thousand bamboos of more than 60 kinds, where you cannot help marvel at the verdure all around.

装饰，产生刚柔相济、动静相衬的效果。也有的地方利用低矮、枝密叶茂的竹种作绿篱、护岸、护坡，以及为花坛道路镶边，另有一番趣味。

setting off the dynamic by the static. Also in some places, people would use dwarf and leafy bamboo as hedge, revetment or for slope protection, or to embroider the flowerbed and road, which looks truly wonderful.

中国三大竹海

　　与其他树种形成的树林相比，竹子一旦成林便很少杂有其他树种，林中甚至没有灌木，再加上竹竿修长，更显雅洁清爽。其他树种的森林大多幽暗深邃，而竹林相对明亮疏朗，而且多临近村舍，使人觉得可亲可近。在中国，大片的竹林常被称为"竹海"，蜀南竹海、宜兴竹海和双溪竹海是著名的三大竹海。

　　蜀南竹海：位于四川省宜宾市长宁和江安县境内。整个竹区面积约120平方公里，其中郁郁葱葱的竹林绵延500多座大小山岭。登高四望，苍山如海，碧涛起伏，是罕见的翠竹海洋。竹林中共有30多个品种的竹子，以楠竹为主。竹庐、竹桥掩映在竹林深处，令人心旷神怡。

　　宜兴竹海：位于江苏省宜兴市区西南的湖㳇镇境内，横跨江苏、浙江、安徽三省，堪称"竹的海洋"。宜兴是中国重要的毛竹产区之一，来到这里但见竹海茫茫，无边无际。

　　双溪竹海：位于浙江省杭州西北的余杭区双溪镇，这里遍地竹林，繁茂苍翠，竹海幽深。

The Three Bamboo Seas in China

Compared with other woods, the bamboo grove, once formed, rarely mixes with other tree species even shrubs. And plus the slender bamboo poles, the grove appears even more elegant and refreshing. While other forests mostly turn out deep and dark, the sparse bamboos rather look bright and amiable as they grow close to the human habitation. In China, a large area of bamboo groves is often referred to as the Bamboo Sea. The three famous bamboo seas are respectively located at southern Sichuan Province, Yixing City in Jiangsu Province and Shuangxi County in Zhejiang Province.

　　Southern Sichuan Bamboo Sea. Located at Changning County and Jiang'an County, in Yibin City, Sichuan Province, this lush Bamboo Sea covers an area of 120 km² stretching over more than

500 mountains of varied sizes. When climbing high and looking around, you can have an eyeful of verdant bamboos undulating upon rolling hills. Besides the widely distributed Nan Bamboo, other 30 varieties also grow in the grove. Bamboo cottages and bamboo bridges nestle deep in the sea. All around is a refreshing scene restful to the spirit.

Yixing Bamboo Sea. It is located at Hufu County southeast of Yixing City in Jiangsu Province and stretches across Jiangsu, Zhejiang and Anhui provinces, hence known as a bamboo sea. Yixing is one of the important Mao Bamboo producing regions in China, where you can see nothing but vast bamboos spreading endlessly.

Shuangxi Bamboo Sea. It is located at Shuangxi County in Yuhang District northwest of Hangzhou City, Zhejiang Province. Phyllostachys bamboo grove here appears lush, deep and serene.

• 蜀南竹海
Bamboo Sea in Southern Sichuan

- 宜兴竹海
  Bamboo Sea in Yixing

- 双溪竹海
  Bamboo Sea in Shuangxi

> 竹之风骨

竹以其岁寒不凋、虚心有节、挺拔正直，赢得了文人士大夫的喜爱，这种喜爱正源于他们内心对君子品德的追求，竹子的自然属性恰好具备了这些特点。竹子有竹节，这个"节"与文人气节的"节"是同一个字，语义相通，所以古人常以竹"有节"来比拟君子之德。所谓气节，是指人们应有的高尚情操，也就是不媚俗，不迎流弊，身处逆境，仍能恪守刚直不阿的人格。在文人眼中，竹子不再是普通的植物，不仅有性格而且有精神，它可以象征坚守节操的君子品格。

爱竹的清代书画家郑板桥曾说："盖竹之体，瘦劲孤高，枝枝傲雪，节节干霄，有君子之豪气凌

> Strong Character of Bamboo

Bamboo does not wither in winter and is also modest and upright, so it enjoys great favor among the literati. They love it because the bamboo's natural properties exactly agree with the gentlemanly virtue they have long pursued. Bamboo has joints, which is the same Chinese character *Jie*, used to laud a scholar's integrity, hence the ancients often use bamboo to symbolize a noble character with high sentiments who will be not vulgar, or subject to improper practices, but scrupulously adhere to moral principles even in adversity. Therefore, in the eyes of the literati, the bamboo is no longer an ordinary plant. It not only has a strong character but a high spirit, and hence can be regarded as an emblem for men of firm integrity.

- 《苏武牧羊图》黄慎（清）
  Painting of Su Wu Tending the Flock, by Huang Shen (Qing Dynasty, 1616-1911)

• 竹叶

竹枝向上生长，竹叶挺直而舒展，显得十分精神。

Bamboo Leaves

The bamboo branches grow upward. The leaves straightly stretch out and hence appear quite perky.

云，不为俗屈。"历代许多仁人志士，被人看作坚守气节的楷模。在他们身上体现的便是一种气节，一种"富贵不能淫，贫贱不能移，威武不能屈"的大丈夫精神。

清代书画家郑板桥是乾隆元年的进士，先后做过山东范县和潍县的知县，晚年主要活动在扬州一带，以诗文书画自适。他为官期间刚正不阿，关心百姓疾苦，将窗下萧萧竹声与百姓的疾苦联系起来，曾

Zheng Banqiao, a remarkable calligrapher and painter in the Qing Dynasty, was himself a bamboo lover. Once he sang highly of the bamboo, saying that with vigorous bearing and aloof dignity it stands against the snow and soars into the sky, just like a gentleman of resolution and ambition who will not bend to the vulgar. In fact, all through the ages, many people with lofty ideals are considered as models of integrity. They embody a national

王子猷爱竹

王子猷，即王徽之，是东晋时期的大书法家王羲之的第五个儿子，也是一位潇洒不羁的名士。据记载，他曾暂住于他人的空房子，当即便命人在房子四周种植竹子。有人问他："你只是暂住一下，又何必种竹子这样麻烦呢？"王子猷指着竹子说："何可一日无此君？"竹子对于他来说已经成了生活中不可缺少的一部分。还有一次王子猷路过吴中，一位士大夫家里有罕见的好竹，他早料到王子猷会来赏竹，便提前早早准备好坐在大厅等着款待他。谁知道王子猷径直去了竹林，欣赏了很长一段时间。主人等得有些焦急，希望王子猷赏竹结束后能够到大厅与他交谈。岂料王子猷竟要直接出门而去，主人急忙喊人关闭大门，王子猷才不得不留下。可见王子猷爱竹爱到了极点。

Wang Ziyou the Bamboo Lover

Wang Huizhi, nicknamed Wang Ziyou, is the fifth son of Wang Xizhi, the great calligrapher of the Eastern Jin Dynasty. Like his father, Wang Huizhi is also a dashing and refined figure. Based on historical records, once he sojourned at other's place yet gave an order to have bamboo planted all around the house. Someone could not understand, asking him why taking so much trouble for a temporary residence. Wang Ziyou pointed to the bamboo and exclaimed, "How can I endure a day without this gentleman?" Indeed, bamboo has become an indispensable part of his life. On another occasion, when Wang Ziyou passed Wuzhong (in today's Jiangsu Province), he saw bamboo of unusual beauty at a scholar's residence. It was within the host's expectation that Ziyou would come to appreciate the bamboo so he had everything well-prepared in advance and sat in the hall waiting to entertain him. However, his guest went straight to the bamboo and enjoyed it for a long time. The host felt a bit anxious, hoping that Wang Ziyou could come to talk with him in the hall afterwards, but it happened that his guest indeed went away directly. The owner hastily asked his servant to close the door and thus kept him back, from which we can see that Wang Ziyou really adores bamboo to the utmost.

在诗中说："衙斋卧听萧萧竹，疑是民间疾苦声。些小吾曹州县吏，一枝一叶总关情。"时值深夜，诗人还没有入睡，听到窗下竹子吹动的声音，便以为是百姓疾苦的声音，可见百姓时时在他心中。虽然是官卑言轻

integrity and the spirit of a real man whom no money and rank can confuse, no poverty and hardship can shake, and no power and force can suffocate.

Zheng Banqiao is a distinguished calligrapher and painter in the Qing Dynasty. In 1736, the first year of

Period Qianlong, he became a successful candidate of the highest imperial examination and was appointed as a magistrate first in Fan County and then in Wei County (today's Weifang City) of Shandong Province. He spent his later years mainly in Yangzhou City, Jiangsu Province, living at ease with poetry, calligraphy and painting. As an upright official, Zheng Banqiao showed deep concern for the masses, and even associated the rustling bamboo at his window with people's well-being. Such sentiment can be traced in one of his poems, "Deep into the night he still could not fall asleep. Lying in the room, the poet heard the rustle of bamboo, and wondered if it was the sobbing of the people." Although a county official inferior in position, still he was thinking about the people all the time and did everything, no matter how trivial it might be, for them with sincerity.

* 《衙斋听竹图》郑板桥（清）
Listening to Bamboo Rustling in the Office, by Zheng Banqiao (Qing Dynasty, 1616-1911)

的州县小吏，但身为地方官的他时刻记挂着百姓，诗中竹子的一枝一叶都与作者的真情有关。

郑板桥一生爱竹、敬竹，创作了大量的以竹为题材的书画作品。他有首《竹石》诗是这样写的："咬定青山不放松，立根原在破岩中。千磨万击还坚劲，任尔东西南北风。"这首诗不止一次被题写在

Throughout his life, Zheng Banqiao held the bamboo in profound esteem and created numerous works with bamboo as subject matter. In the poem *Bamboo and Stone*, he draws a sharp image of deep bamboo roots that bite into the jagged mountain stones; no matter how hard the gale blows, despite any strike of storms, they will never let go. Actually he was very pleased with this poem and

- 《竹子笋石图》郑板桥（清）
  Bamboos, Shoots and Rocks, by Zheng Banqiao (Qing Dynasty, 1616-1911)

•《竹石图》郑板桥（清）
Bamboo and Stone, by Zheng Banqiao (Qing Dynasty, 1616-1911)

他所画的墨竹上，可见他对此诗的满意之情。"咬定"用拟人化的手法写出了竹子的坚定，不动摇，不放松，它的根深深地扎在陡峭不平的岩石中间，把它恶劣的生存环境呈现在我们的面前。长在崎岖不平的破岩中的竹，是山野中的竹子，

more than once inscribed it on his ink bamboo paintings. By the word "Bite", he personifies the bamboo as firm and resolute to root deep in the jagged broken rocks. Thus the poet presents its harsh living environment, and reveals us that the bamboo he portrays is not planted in the courtyard but grows in the mountain.

无竹令人俗

宋代大诗人苏轼曾说:"宁可食无肉,不可居无竹。无肉令人瘦,无竹令人俗。人瘦尚可肥,士俗不可医。"思意是:饭菜中可以没有肉,但是居所附近不能没有竹子,饭菜中没有肉会让人身体瘦下来,但是没有竹子就会让人变得庸俗。人瘦了尚且还能胖起来,但是如果士人俗了便不可医了。

传说苏轼十分喜欢肉食,至今还流传着一道与他有关的名菜——"东坡肘子"。就是这样一位美食家,都说宁可不吃肉,也要有竹子,可见在苏轼生活的北宋时代,士人居必有竹,已经成为一种生活风尚。

Life Without Bamboo is Vulgar

Su Shi, the great poet in the Northern Song Dynasty, once wrote, "I can eat without meat, yet I can't live without bamboo. The former only makes me fleshless; but the latter renders me vulgar. A thin person can be fat again, but a vulgar man is really beyond cure."

According to the legend, Su Shi was very fond of meat. The famous dish Dongpo Pork now circulated is precisely named after him. That even such a gourmet would rather to eat without meat than live without bamboo, aptly illustrates that to live with bamboo has become a lifestyle for the literati of the Northern Song Dynasty.

- 《竹石图轴》朱耷(清)
Painting Scroll of Bamboo and Rock, by Zhu Da (Qing Dynasty, 1616-1911)

而非庭院中所栽种的竹。如果说前两句还是在写自然之竹，那么"千磨万击还坚劲，任尔东西南北风"则道出了竹的坚韧与毫无畏惧的精神，无论什么样的摧残，竹依然以挺拔如故的风姿呈现在人们眼前。自古以来，咏竹诗俯拾皆是，但是能把竹不屈的风骨写到最动人的程度，此诗当仁不让。

If the first two lines mainly focus on the natural bamboo, it seems that the last two lines rather point out its tough and fearless spirit; or more specifically, despite any kind of ravage, the bamboo still retains its grace, standing tall and upright. Ode to bamboo can be found everywhere in all ages, yet this is the only one that best bring out its stubborn and unyielding character.

- 《墨竹图》郑板桥（清）

郑板桥笔下的墨竹，枝干挺拔，寥寥数笔，形神兼备，瘦劲坚韧、豪迈凌空之风骨毕现。

Ink Bamboo, by Zheng Banqiao (Qing Dynasty, 1616-1911)

Zheng Banqiao's ink bamboo painting has upright branches. By a few strokes, he already reveals its vigor, loftiness and strength of character simultaneously with unity in form and spirit.

> 竹之生活

中国人很早便开始利用竹子这种植物了。关于竹的实用性，北宋文豪苏轼一言以蔽之："食者竹笋，庇者竹瓦，载者竹筏，爨者竹薪，衣者竹皮，书者竹纸，履者竹鞋。"竹可以食用，可以用作建筑材料，可以制作交通工具，可以用来烧火做饭，可以做衣服鞋子，还可以做书写材料，其用途可以说涉及中国人生活的方方面面。

根据《诗经》《尚书·禹贡》等文献记载，竹笋在西周时期已成为佳肴，时至今日竹笋仍是中国人餐桌上的重要食材。竹笋一年四季皆有，但唯有春笋、冬笋味道最佳。烹调时无论是凉拌、煎炒还是熬汤，均鲜嫩清香，是人们喜欢的佳肴之一。竹笋不仅味道鲜美，

> Bamboo's Life

Chinese have long begun to make use of bamboos. Su Shi, an eminent writer in the Northern Song Dynasty once briefly summarized its practicality as follows: People can eat bamboo shoots, have bamboo as building materials for shelter and means of transportation, or use it to cook dinners, make clothes and shoes, or simply as writing material. In short, it nearly involves all aspects of the Chinese life.

As recorded in the *Book of Songs* and chapter *Tribute of Yu* in the *Classic of History*, bamboo shoots have become a delicacy early in the Western Zhou Dynasty and still serve as important ingredients of the Chinese dinner up to the present. People can enjoy bamboo shoots all year round, but only those produced in spring and winter taste the best. No matter as cold dish, fried or

- 竹笋
  Bamboo Shoots

- 鲜美的油焖竹笋
  Delicious Braised Bamboo Shoots

而且含有丰富的蛋白质和磷、铁、钙、镁等微量元素，纤维素的含量也很高，食之可以促进肠道蠕动，帮助消化，去积食，防便秘。

除了为人们提供直接食用的竹笋之外，竹子还以自身特有的清香，成为中国人饭桌上独特的风景。如湘菜中著名的"粉蒸竹筒鱼"，就是将鲜鱼与炒过的糯米及各种调料一起放入竹筒中，上锅蒸熟。完成后鱼肉不仅鲜嫩，而且带有竹子的清香，柔软味美，别有风味。

made into soup, bamboo shoots look all fresh and tender and become one of people's favorites. Indeed, they are not only delicious, but contain rich protein and trace elements such as phosphorus, iron, calcium, magnesium, etc. Besides, bamboo shoots also show high cellulose content, which can promote intestinal peristalsis, facilitate digestion, eliminate retention of food and prevent constipation.

Bamboo not only provides people with edible bamboo shoots, but is used by the Chinese to refine other dishes

• 竹筒饭
Bamboo-tube Rice

　　此外，还有在云南、贵州一带十分流行的竹筒饭。男人们进山砍柴或打猎，野炊时随手砍一截青竹，将随身携带的大米淘洗干净后放在竹筒中，加水，用芭蕉叶塞好筒口，吊在火堆上烧烤至熟。取下后将竹筒竖劈为两半，就可食用，米香与竹香混合，令人齿颊留香。

　　竹林中还生长着一种珍贵的食

because of its unique fragrance. For instance, Steamed Fish with Sticky Rice in Bamboo Tube is well-known in Hunan cuisine. People put the fresh fish, fried sticky rice and various spices together into the bamboo tube and then steam it in the pot. Fish thus cooked not only tastes fresh, soft and delicious, but with bamboo fragrance and thus of distinctive flavor.

Bamboo rice is also very popular in

用菌——竹荪。这是寄生在枯竹根部的一种隐花菌类，一般于秋季生长在潮湿的竹林地，它有深绿色的菌帽，雪白色圆柱状的菌柄，在菌柄顶端有一围细致洁白的网状裙从菌盖向下铺开，因此被称为"雪裙仙子""真菌之花"。由于生长条件相当苛刻，成长不易，得之更难，竹荪历来被认为是珍奇之物，曾被作为贡品专供皇室食用。竹荪不仅味道异常鲜美，而且含有丰富的营养成分。

Yunnan Province and Guizhou Province. When men go to mountains for firewood or hunting, they usually carry rice with them. For meal, they will cut a length of bamboo, wash the rice and put it in the bamboo tube, then add water, use plantain leaves to stuff the ends of the tube, and finally hang it over fire. When it is thoroughly cooked, they will split the tube vertically in two and then enjoy the soft rice of bamboo flavor, which is really yummy with a lingering aftertaste.

In the bamboo grove, you can also find a rare edible mushroom called *Zhusun* in Chinese. This cryptogamic fungus is parasitic on withered bamboo and usually springs up in autumn on the wet ground of a bamboo grove. It features a dark green cap and a snow-white cylindrical stipe. On the top of the stipe is a circle of delicate white reticulate skirt outspread from the cap, so *Zhusun* is also known as Fairy with Snowy Skirt or Flower of the Fungus. Since it lives in very harsh environment and very few can survive, *Zhusun* has long been considered a rarity and once served as a tribute specifically for the imperial family. It not only tastes extraordinary but has rich nutrients.

● 竹荪
Zhusun

- **傣家竹楼**

竹楼是傣族人世代居住的居所，属于干栏式建筑。四方形的竹楼底层架空，没有墙壁，专供饲养牲畜和堆放杂物。楼上有堂屋和卧室。堂屋设火塘，是烧茶做饭和家人团聚的地方。外有开敞的前廊和晒台。前廊是白天工作、吃饭、休息和接待客人的地方，既明亮又通风；晒台是盥洗、晒衣、晾晒农作物和存放水罐的地方。这一廊一台是竹楼不可缺少的部分。这样的竹楼四面通风，可避虫兽侵袭，冬暖夏凉。而且当地每年雨量集中，洪水频发，竹楼楼下架空，墙又为多空隙的竹篾，利于洪水通过。

Bamboo House of the Dai People

For generations the Dai people live in the bamboo house supported by wooden poles. The first floor of this square building rises upon stilts without walls, mainly for raising livestock or as storage. Both the main room and the bedroom are at the upper story. There is a fireplace in the central room, where the family will join around to make tea or cook dinners. Outside builds a front porch and also a balcony. The front porch is bright and airy, where people work, eat, rest or receive guests during the day. The balcony, however, is a place for washing, drying clothes or crops, and storing pitchers. Both are indispensable parts of a bamboo house. Such a structure is not only well-ventilated, but resists pest or animal invasion, cool in summer and warm in winter. Besides, as local tropical climate brings concentrated rainfall every year that causes frequent flooding, the bamboo house built on stilts with bamboo-woven walls is quite conductive to the passage of the flood.

竹子体轻质坚，皮厚中空，抗弯拉力强，极为坚韧，是不可多得的建筑材料。中国人将竹子用于建筑的历史特别悠久。早在汉代就有关于竹子建造房屋的记载，能工巧匠曾利用竹子为汉武帝建造了美丽的甘泉祠宫。宋代大学士王禹偁

Bamboo is thick-skinned and hollow inside, which makes it light yet extremely tough with bending resistance, and hence a rare building material. Chinese people have used bamboo in construction for a particularly long time. Early in the Han Dynasty (206 B.C.-220 B.C.), there had been records on bamboo houses.

曾自造竹楼，还撰写了《黄州新建小竹楼记》，对竹楼的妙处津津乐道。至今在南方还能见到不少竹楼，尤其是在西南少数民族聚居区，这些竹楼极富民族特色，绿树芭蕉之中，掩映着美丽的竹楼，充满诗情画意。

竹子在建筑装饰方面的用途也十分广泛。北京故宫东北角的宁寿宫中，有座别具江南风格的倦勤斋。倦勤斋内部随处可见竹子的影

Craftsmen once built the magnificent Ganquan Palace for Emperor Wudi of the Han Dynasty, using sheer bamboo. Wang Yuchen, a great scholar of the Northern Song Dynasty once built a bamboo house all by himself. In the essay *Bamboo Pavilion in Huanggang* he extolled its beauty with great relish. Even today there are lots of bamboo houses in southern China, especially in the southwest regions inhabited by ethnic groups. These bamboo houses outshine with distinctive

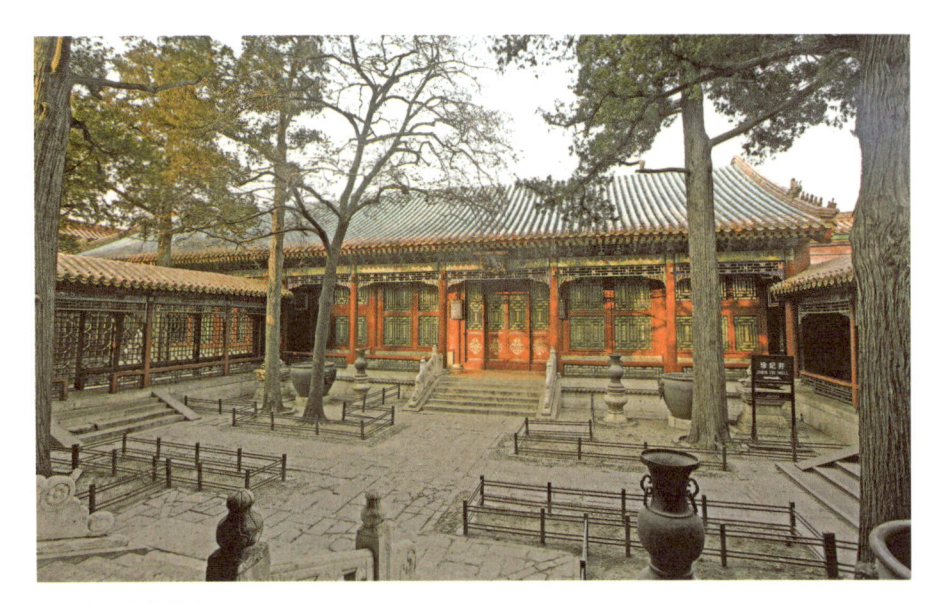

- **北京故宫倦勤斋**
在倦勤斋100多平方米的空间里，四处都是精美的竹编工艺品，床和书架也有竹丝镶嵌和雕刻。
Juanqin Zhai (Diligent Service) in the Imperial Palace in Beijing
It is over 100 m² in space and almost filled with fine bamboo woven artifacts. Even the bed and the bookshelf are decorated with bamboo mosaic and carving.

● 湖北云梦睡虎地出土的秦朝竹简

1975年，湖北云梦县睡虎地的秦代墓葬中出土了1000余支秦代竹简，这些竹简长23.1—27.8厘米，宽0.5—0.8厘米，内文为墨书秦篆，绝大部分属于法律制度的内容。

Inscribed Bamboo Slips of the Qin Dynasty (221 B.C.-206 B.C.) Unearthed at Shuihudi Tomb in Yunmeng County, Hubei Province.

In 1975, more than 1,000 bamboo slips were excavated at this tomb. They are generally 23.1-27.8 cm long and 0.5-0.8 cm wide. The text was all written in ink by the ancient style of calligraphy adopted in the Qin Dynasty, mostly concerned with the legal system of that time.

子，其最大特色便是使用了"竹丝镶嵌"这种装饰工艺。倦勤斋所有的门扇均由紫檀木雕刻而成，而图案里填的都是竹丝，称为"竹丝镶嵌"，图案中间还嵌着数百块玉石。倦勤斋内壁是紫檀木，外面贴以翻黄（又称"贴黄"，即取用竹子内壁黄色表层，劈片、整平、软化，在上面刻饰山水、花鸟、人物等）或镶嵌装饰。

中国传统文房辅助用具中，也有很多集精美工艺与观赏性于一身的器具是由竹子做成的。比如，有"文房四宝"之称的毛笔以及书画

ethnic features, shaded in the lush plantains and full of artistic sentiment.

Bamboo is also widely used in decoration of the building. In the *Ningshou Gong* (Palace of Tranquil Longevity), northeast of the Imperial Palace in Beijing, there stands the *Juanqin Zhai* (Diligent Service) of unique Southern Style (style south of the Yangtze River). The shadow of bamboo extends to every corner by means of this remarkable decorative technique, mosaic of bamboo filament. To be specific, all the doors and windows of the *Juanqin Zhai* are rosewood first carved with various designs and then filled in with

用的宣纸都有竹子的成分。中国在造纸术发明之前，竹简曾是重要的书写材料。

中国以竹子来制造毛笔的历史也非常悠久。1954年在湖南长沙左家公山一座战国时期的木椁墓中就出土过一支兔毫毛笔，其笔管便是实心的竹子。到了唐代，随着社会的繁荣和文化教育的发展，毛

• 斑竹兔毫笔（元）
Writing Brush of Rabbit Hair and Mottled Bamboo Shaft (Yuan Dynasty, 1206-1368)

bamboo filament as well as hundred pieces of jade. The inner walls all have rosewood as material pasted with veneered bamboo carving (*Tiehuang* or *Fanhuang* in Chinese, which takes out the yellow inner-wall surface of bamboo, then splits, flattens, softens it, and finally carves landscape, flower, bird, figure and other decorative patterns upon it).

In traditional China, bamboo is also adopted to make certain stationeries of fine craftsmanship and high ornamental value. For instance, the writing brush, known as one of the Four Treasures of the Study, as well as the rice paper used in calligraphy and painting all have bamboo as ingredient. Before the invention of paper, bamboo even served as important writing material in ancient China.

China has a long history in making bamboo brushes. In 1954, a writing brush of rabbit hair and solid bamboo was unearthed from a wooden-chambered tomb of the Warring States Period (475B.C.-221B.C.) at Zuojiagong Mountain in Changsha City, Hunan Province. When it came to the Tang Dynasty (618-907), social prosperity, cultural and educational development rendered the writing brush rather inseparable from the literati. And moreover, both in quantity and quality,

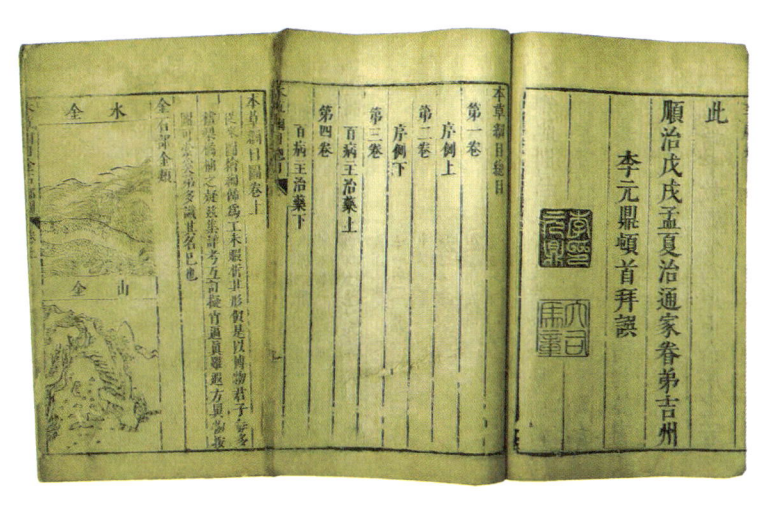

● 竹纸古籍
Ancient Book of Bamboo Paper

笔成为文人时刻不可离身的书写工具。此时毛笔的制作，无论在数量上还是质量上都达到了前所未有的水平。尤其是湖州、宣州所产的毛笔，以湘妃竹、金竹等名贵竹材制笔杆，工艺高超，颇负盛名。唐代著名的文学家韩愈写有《毛颖传》，颂扬毛笔的功绩，盛赞毛笔的品格，封毛笔为"管城子"。明代画家文震亨特别喜欢斑竹，他认为以斑竹做的笔杆是最雅致的，他在《长物志》中说："古有金银管、象管、玳瑁管、玻璃管、镂金、绿沉管，近有紫檀、雕花诸管，俱俗不可用，惟斑管最雅，不则竟用白

writing brush reached its heyday in production. Especially those made of valuable varieties such as Xiangfei bamboo and gold bamboo exemplified superb skill and enjoyed great fame in Huzhou and Xuanzhou. Han Yu (768-824), the great man of letters in the Tang Dynasty named the writing brush as *Guanchengzi* in the *Biography of Mao Ying*, celebrated its achievements and praised its character to a great extent. Wen Zhenheng, a great Chinese painter in the Ming Dynasty was particularly fond of mottled bamboo and considered brush shaft made of it the most elegant. In *The Element of Garden Making*, he thought all penholders made of gold, silver, ivory,

竹。"白竹就是有"笔管竹"之称的箬竹和苦竹。

竹子也可以用来制作纸张，四川的竹纸就很有名。竹纸制造技艺以当年生嫩毛竹为原料。明代科学家宋应星在《天工开物》中写道："用竹麻者为竹纸，精者极其洁白，供书文、印文、柬启用。"

tortoiseshell, glass, gilded carving and dark green-lacquered materials in ancient times or modern ones of rosewood with carved patterns are vulgar and do not write well. Indeed, he singled out the penholder made of mottled bamboo and the fargesia semicoriacea above all. The latter is also known as Brush Shaft Bamboo, mainly including indocalamus and bitter bamboo.

The paper can also be made from bamboo. Sichuan Province is particularly famous for its bamboo paper which has tender new Mao bamboo as raw material. Song Yingxing, a Chinese scientist in the Ming Dynasty once related in the *Exploitation of the Works of Nature*, that a fine bamboo paper is spotlessly white, suitable for writing and sealing texts, notes or letters.

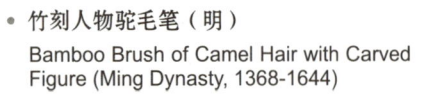

• 竹刻人物驼毛笔（明）
Bamboo Brush of Camel Hair with Carved Figure (Ming Dynasty, 1368-1644)

罄竹难书

罄竹难书是人们经常用到的成语之一,其字面的意思是把山上的竹子都制成竹简,也难以书写完罪行,形容人作恶多端、劣迹斑斑。这个成语出自《旧唐书·李密传》:"罄南山之竹,书罪未穷。"大约在春秋时代,以竹片串联而成的竹简诞生了,成为造纸术发明之前最主要的书写材料。人们把竹子削成狭长的竹片,叫作"简",再把若干的简编缀在一起,便成为记事著书的"册"(策)了。

Too Numerous to Record

This frequently used idiom literally means that misdeeds are too much to write down even if you cut down all bamboos. It first appeared in the *Biography of Li Mi* in the *Old Book of the Tang Dynasty* that said the innumerable evils might exhaust all bamboo in the southern mountains. Early in the Spring and Autumn Period, the bamboo slips already came into being and remained the dominant writing material till the invention of paper. People shaved the bamboo into slender slips and then strung them together for recording or writing.

• 竹简(战国)(图片提供:FOTOE)
Inscribed Bamboo Slips (Warring States Period, 475 B.C.-221 B.C.)

• 竹雕镇纸（近代）
Bamboo Paperweight with Carved Design (Modern Times)

• 竹雕笔筒（清）
Bamboo Brush Pot with Carved Design (Qing Dynasty, 1616-1911)

　　此外，在古代文人的书房中，笔筒、臂搁、镇纸也多由竹子做成，备受文人喜爱。臂搁也称"腕枕"，一般是用去节的竹筒分劈成三片，上面多雕以浅刻平雕，刻制书画、名言警句一类，是文房书案上的重要饰物，也是文人比较喜爱的把玩之物。古代的文人墨客在炎炎夏日挥毫时将竹臂搁放于手臂下，可以防止所出的汗洇湿纸面。另外竹子性凉，枕在手下很清爽，

　　Besides, in the ancient study some brush pots, arm rests, and paperweights are also made of bamboo and enjoy special favor among the scholars. The arm rest, also known as wrist pillow, usually splits a jointless bamboo tube into three, then decorates with shallow carving, or engraves calligraphy, painting or famous aphorism thereupon. Thus it ornaments the writing desk and also becomes one of scholars' favorite play things. The ancient literati usually rest

有情趣的文人自然爱不释手，臂搁也便有了"竹夫人"的雅称。

their arms on it when writing in the summer heat, and thus prevent the sweat soaking the paper. Moreover, as the bamboo is cool in nature, it feels quite refreshing, so some scholars of good taste are very passionate about it. The arm rest is also vividly referred to as "Bamboo Lady" therefore.

In addition to the bamboo rest, the carved bamboo brush pot is another essential object on the writing desk of the Ming and Qing dynasties. The bamboo brush pots now collected in the Palace

- 透雕荷叶纹竹笔筒（清）
  Bamboo Brush Pot with Openwork of Lotus Leaves Design (Qing Dynasty, 1616-1911)

- 留青花鸟纹竹雕臂搁（清）
  "留青"就是留用竹子表面的一层青皮雕刻花纹，铲去花纹以外的青皮，露出皮下的竹肌作为底子，青皮干后会逐渐由白转为嫩黄，竹肌则会由浅黄经深黄而转为红紫。
  Liuqing Bamboo Arm Rest with Flower and Bird Design (Qing Dynasty, 1616-1911)
  Liuqing technique is to retain the surface green skin of the bamboo and carve patterns onto it, then remove the rest skin and expose the bamboo muscle as background. When dry, the green skin will turn from white to yellow, while the yellow bamboo muscle will deepen into reddish purple in color.

• 竹雕臂搁
Bamboo Arm Rest with Carved Design

除了臂搁，竹雕笔筒也是明清书案上必不可少的物件。现在藏于故宫博物院的竹笔筒或浮雕、或圆雕、或浅刻、或留青，都精美至极。除去笔筒，还有单独作为摆设的竹雕摆件、竹雕笔洗等，竹刻工艺之美令人叹为观止。

Museum are extremely delicate. Some of them are in relief, some in circular or shallow carving, and others adopt *Liuqing* technique (as explained a few lines below). Apart from the brush pot, bamboo carved ornaments and brush washers also manifest great expertise and are breathtaking in appearance.

《天工开物》中记载的竹纸制法

《天工开物》是中国古代一部综合性的科学技术著作，成书于明代崇祯十年（1637年），作者是明末的科学家宋应星。全书叙述了各种农作物和工业原料的种类、产地、生产技术和工艺装备，被称为"中国17世纪的工艺百科全书"。书中详细记载了用竹子造纸的工艺过程，共有5个步骤：

1.斩竹漂塘：斩下嫩竹放入池中浸泡百日以上。
2.煮楻足火：将泡好的竹子放入桶内与石灰一道蒸煮八日八夜。

3.荡料入帘：将打烂的竹料倒入水槽内，并以竹帘在水中荡料，竹料成为薄层附于竹帘上面。

    4.覆帘压纸：将竹帘翻过去，使湿纸落于板上，即成一张纸。如此重复，使一张张湿纸叠积上千，然后上加木板重压，挤去水分。

    5.透火焙干：将湿纸逐张揭开，贴在土砖砌成的夹巷墙上，巷中生火，将湿纸焙干。

Bamboo Paper Making Method Documented in *Exploitation of the Works of Nature*

Exploitation of the Works of Nature is a miscellaneous work on ancient Chinese science and technology written by Song Yingxing in the tenth year (1637) the Period Chongzhen of the Ming Dynasty. The book refers to various species of crops and industrial raw materials and records their place of origin, production technique and processing equipment, hence known as the Technical Encyclopedia of the 17th Century China. Particularly it documents in detail the process of bamboo paper making, five steps in total as follows:

1. Cut and Soak: Cut down the tender bamboo and soak it in the pool for hundred days or more.
2. Stew with Lime: Put the well-soaked bamboo into a barrel. Stew it with lime for eight days and eight nights.
3. Sweep the Mash: Pour the bamboo mash into a tank, sweep it over with a bamboo screen, and then a thin layer of bamboo material will attach to the screen.
4. Turn and Press: Turn over the screen so that the wet paper can fall onto a board. Then repeat the process over and again, till thousands of pieces accumulate to a thick pile. Squeeze the water out by a heavy wood.
5. Bake and Dry: Take off the wet paper piece by piece. Attach them to the brick walls on both sides of the lane. Make a fire to dry the wet paper.

• 《天工开物》插图——斩竹漂塘
Illustration in *Exploitation of the Works of Nature*: Cut and Soak

- 《天工开物》插图——煮楻足火
Illustration in *Exploitation of the Works of Nature*: Stew with Lime

- 《天工开物》插图——荡料入帘
Illustration in *Exploitation of the Works of Nature*: Sweep the Mash

- 《天工开物》插图——覆帘压纸
Illustration in *Exploitation of the Works of Nature*: Turn and Press

- 《天工开物》插图——透火焙干
Illustration In *Exploitation of the Works of Nature*: Bake and Dry

• 竹笛
Bamboo Flute

竹还是中华民族乐器的重要制作材料，被列为中国古代乐器分类的"八音"之一，"丝竹"成为音乐的代称。笙笛、洞箫、云箫等传统乐器均用竹制成。竹制乐器体现了中华民族对待自然的"天人合一"或"天人协调"的态度，显示了中国传统音乐简明、灵活的特征。

笛子由一根中空去节的竹管做成，笛身上开有若干小孔，通过演奏者吹入气流使管内空气振动而发音。笛子的表现力非常丰富，既能演奏悠长、婉转的旋律，又能表现欢快华丽的曲调。

箫与笛外形很像，不过箫为竖吹，管身只有音孔而没有膜孔，音色柔美圆润、幽远典雅，内蕴贵族气质，为历代文人墨客所钟爱。

Besides, bamboo is also an important material for making musical instruments. Traditional Chinese musical instruments are classified into eight groups, called Eight *Yin*. Bamboo woodwind instrument is one of them, which together with the

• 《吹箫图》唐寅（明）
Painting of Lady Blowing Xiao, by Tang Yin (Ming Dynasty, 1368-1644)

笙由若干竹管插在木制或铜制的带有吹孔的笙斗上制成，竹管中装有铜制的簧片。吹奏时用手指按住竹管下端的开孔，使簧片与管中气柱发生共鸣，即可发出乐音。其音色明亮甜美，清越柔和。

- 吹笙女子砖雕（五代）
Brick with carved design of lady blowing *Sheng* (Five Dynasties, 907-960)

stringed instrument becomes a synonym for music, as *Sizhu*. *Sheng* (free-reed pipe), bamboo flute, *Dongxiao* and *Yunxiao* are all made of bamboo. This not only reflects the well-known Chinese philosophy of harmony between man and nature, but also reveals the simple and flexible features of traditional Chinese music.

Flute is a jointless and hollow bamboo tube with a number of holes on it. In performance the player will blow to vibrate the air inside and thus make a sound. The flute can produce rich effects, such as a long and graceful melody, or a cheerful and gorgeous tune.

Similar to the flute in shape, *Xiao* is only blown vertically. It has sound holes but no membrane holes. The tone is usually soft and mellow, deep and elegant, of aristocratic flavor, and therefore beloved by scholars since ancient times.

Sheng is to insert a number of bamboo pipes equipped with copper reeds onto a wooden or copper round base that has a blowing hole. In performance, the player will press the holes in the lower end of the pipe with fingers and blow to make the reed and the air column within resonate. The tone of *Sheng* is light and sweet, clear and soft.

抖空竹

空竹是中国传统的民间玩具，出现于明代，北京、天津等地最为流行。清代的《燕京杂记》载："京师儿童，有抖空竹之戏。"空竹有单轮和双轮之分。制作时，选多年生毛竹锯成竹筒，上封以木片，用松香、苎麻填满缝隙，并在外面缠上数道以使其牢固，在竹筒上雕出风口，然后在两个竹筒间用梨木或蜡杆作轴，调整平衡后便告完成。玩时用两根竹棍拴上麻绳，绳的长短可根据手臂的长短来定，将空竹放在麻绳上，用手来回牵动竹棍，带动空竹旋转。当速度很快时，空竹便能发出嗡嗡的响声。抖空竹时需要双臂用力、反复开合，有益于增强肺活量和锻炼臂力，因而是一种很有趣味的健身玩具。清代以来，抖空竹已发展成为受欢迎的杂技节目，艺人们创造出许多新的花样和高难技巧，表演时配合音乐和优美的舞姿，极具观赏性。

Diabolo

Diabolo or devil on two sticks is a traditional folk toy in China that first emerged in the Ming Dynasty, and is most popular in Beijing and Tianjin. As recorded in the *Miscellany of Beijing* in the Qing Dynasty, children in the capital liked playing diabolo tricks. The diabolo can be single-wheeled or double-wheeled. People usually select perennial Mao bamboo as making material, saw it into tubes, seal the ends with wood chips, fill the aperture with rosin and ramie, and wrap around many times to make it firm. Then carve an air hole on the two tubes, use pear wood or wax rod as axis between them and finally adjust to keep balance. To play with it, people have a string fastened on two bamboo sticks. The length of the string can vary with that of one's arms. They place the diabolo on the string, pulling the sticks back and forth to rotate the diabolo. While tossed fast enough, the devil can make a buzzing sound. Besides, as the game demands repeated movement of the arms, it helps to improve lung capacity and develop the arm muscle, therefore both interesting and heath-building. Since the Qing Dynasty, diabolo playing has developed into a popular acrobatic show. Artists create a lot of new tricks and highly difficult skills which combined with music and the graceful body movement, make a great spectacle.

- 单轮空竹与双轮空竹
Single-wheeled Diabolo and Double-wheeled Diabolo

> 墨竹潇洒

在中国画的花鸟画体系中，墨竹是很重要的一个画种。在古代文人的心目中，画竹可以养胸中浩然之气，竹子的性格可以潜移默化地影响、启发作画的人，这是画家们爱画墨竹的重要原因。

北宋时期，四川省绵阳市盐亭县出了一位大诗人、大画家，名叫文同。他爱竹成痴，而且酷爱画竹，在自家宅前种了很多竹子，每天观察竹子。他不断钻研竹子在春夏秋冬四季有什么变化；在阴晴雨雪天，竹子的颜色、姿势又有什么不同；在强烈的阳光照耀下和在明净的月光映照下，竹子又有什么两样；不同品种的竹子，又有哪些不同……因此文同画出的竹子各具形态，栩栩如生。他画竹叶以浓墨为

> Natural Charm of Ink Bamboo

Ink bamboo constitutes a crucial part in the system of Chinese flower-and-bird painting. In the eyes of ancient literati, bamboo painting can help to nurture a noble spirit, unconsciously influence the artist in character and inspire his creation. Hence a great many scholars are dedicated to ink bamboo painting.

In the Northern Song Dynasty (960-1127), a great poet and painter, Wen Tong was born in Yanting County, Mianyang City, Sichuan Province. His passion for bamboo manifests both in the painting and in his residence. Indeed he planted many bamboos in front of his house, observed them every day and sought to figure out their variation in the four seasons: whether their color and posture would change in different weathers, whether they would be any

- 《墨竹图》文同（北宋）

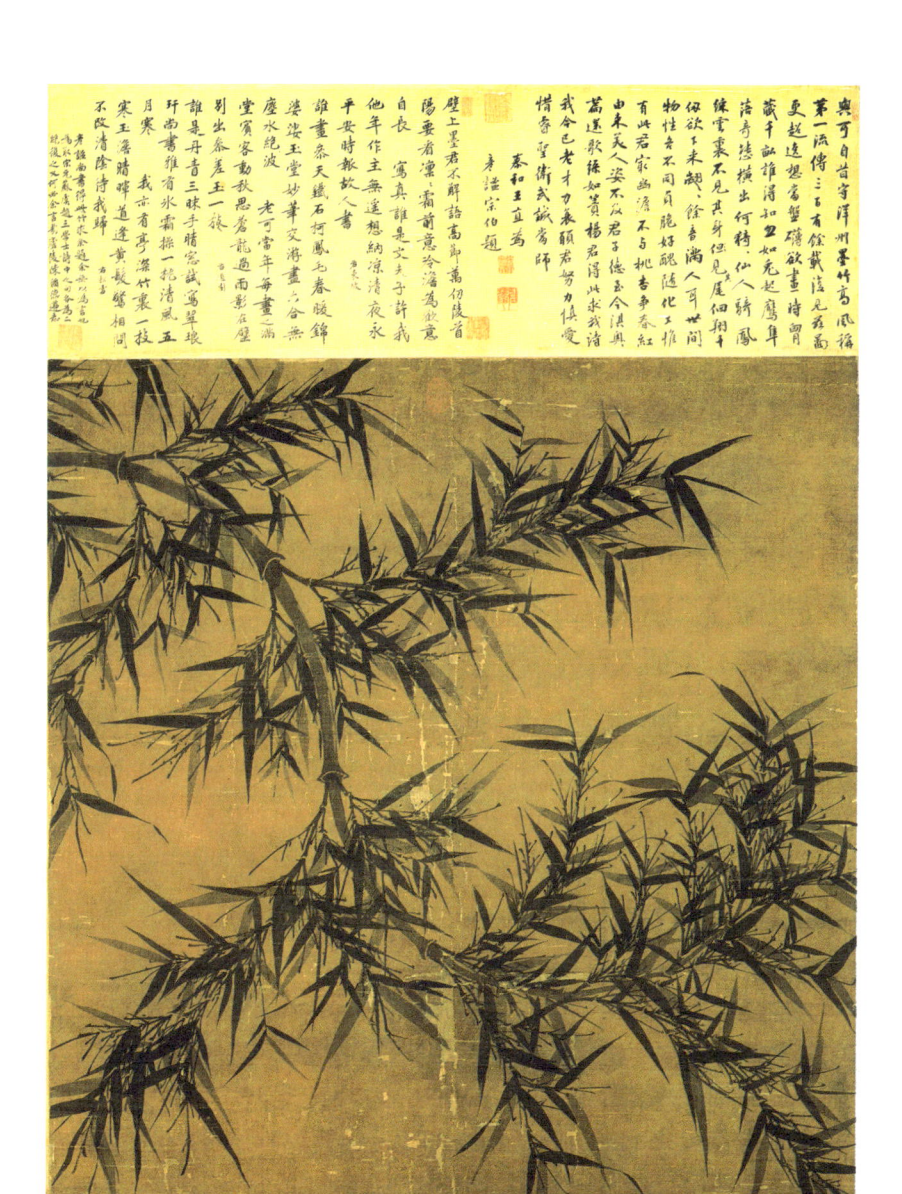

  文同曾说："意有所不适而无所遣之，故一发而为竹。"他画竹是为了抒发心中不适之意。

  Ink Bamboo Painting, by Wen Tong (Northern Song Dynasty, 960-1127)

  As Wen Tong himself once claimed, he painted bamboo mainly to vent the discomfort in heart.

面，淡墨为背，不施勾勒，创造了一笔写成的"没骨"画竹之法。他画的墨竹枝伸叶立，如出绢纸。传说他画在墙上的竹子，连麻雀都会信以为真，纷纷飞去停歇。大文学家苏轼曾赞其画竹之法，说他"画竹必先得成竹于胸中"。汉语中常见的成语"胸有成竹"就从此而来。文同开启了画坛著名的"湖州竹派"。后世各代出现了不少墨竹画名家，或多或少都受到文同墨竹画法的影响。

- 《竹石图》柯九思（元）

Bamboo and Rock, by Ke Jiusi (Yuan Dynasty, 1206-1368)

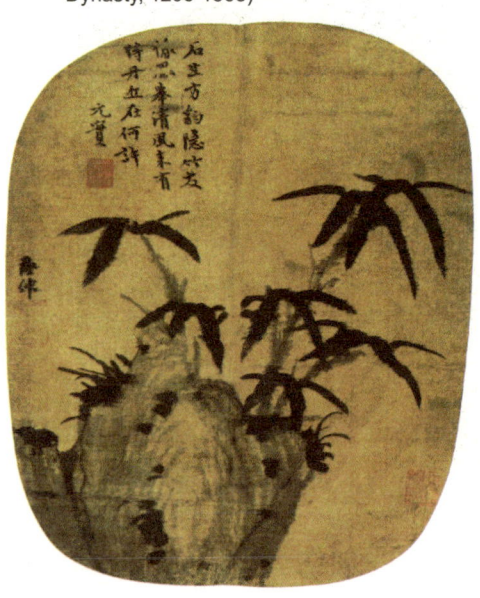

different in the strong sunlight and in the clear moonshine, or how different species of bamboo varied from each other. As a result, bamboos under his brush are all lifelike and of particular forms. Heavy ink in the front, light ink in the back, the leaves are not outlined but depicted in a boneless style. The branches stretch out with vigor as if to break open the framework. As one legend goes, his bamboo was so vivid on the wall that even the sparrows took it as real and would fly to perch on it. Su Shi, the great man of letters once spoke highly of his bamboo painting skills, saying that he must have well thought the image out in the mind before setting it onto paper. The famous Chinese idiom, having a well-drawn bamboo in mind (meaning have a well-thought-out plan), just comes from this story. Wen Tong also founded the Huzhou Bamboo School well-known in the painting circle. Many famous ink bamboo painters of later generations are all influenced by his painting technique to a certain extent.

Ke Jiusi, a distinguished calligrapher and painter of the Yuan Dynasty, was especially good at ink bamboo painting. Moreover, he inherited and further developed Wen Tong's technique and integrated Chinese calligraphy into painting in a strikingly

柯九思是元代著名的书画家。他尤善画墨竹，并且发展了墨竹画鼻祖文同的画法，别开生面地将中国古代书法融于画法之中。柯九思笔下的墨竹"各具姿态，曲尽生意"，新竹拔地而起，枝茂叶盛，欣欣向荣；幼竹奋发向上，充满朝气；老竹稍稍倚斜，枝叶扶疏，劲节健骨。明朝刘伯温、清朝乾隆皇帝对柯九思的墨竹都有题咏之作。

new way. His ink bamboos all feature particular gesture and enormous vitality. The new bamboos shoot up, flourishing with luxuriant foliage; the seedlings strive to grow upward, full of vigor; the aged ones incline gently yet stand firm and energetic, with leaves and branches exuberant yet well-spaced. Liu Bowen, a Chinese minister in the Ming Dynasty and Emperor Qianlong of the Qing Dynasty all paid tribute to his ink bamboos.

岁寒三友

坚忍不拔的青松，挺拔多姿的翠竹，傲雪报春的冬梅，这三种植物虽系不同属科，却都有不畏严霜的特性。它们在岁寒中同生，历来被中国古今文人所喜爱，誉为"岁寒三友"。关于"岁寒三友"的来历，据说在北宋神宗年间，文学家苏轼被贬到黄州（今湖北黄冈），初到黄州时，生活上产生了困难，他便向黄州府讨来了数十亩荒地，开垦种植，借以改善生活。苏轼在这块地上种了稻、麦等农作物，又筑园围墙，造起房屋来。他将房子取名"雪堂"，在屋内的四壁都画上雪花，还在园子里遍植松、柏、竹、梅等花木。一年春天，黄州知州徐君猷来雪堂看望他，打趣道："你这房间起居睡卧，环顾侧看处处是雪。当真天寒飘雪、人迹难至时，不觉得太冷清吗？"苏轼手指院内花木，爽朗笑道："风泉两部乐，松竹三益友。"意为风声和泉声就是可解寂寞的两部乐章，枝叶常青的松柏、经冬不凋的竹子和傲霜开放的梅花，就是可伴冬寒的三位益友。

Three Friends in Chilly Winter

The persevering pine, the tall and fair bamboo, and the sturdy wintry plum that blossoms against the heavy snow to harbinger spring, although they come from different genera, yet all defy severe cold. They all endure the adverse winter fearlessly, hence enjoy great favor among Chinese scholars throughout the history and are even honored as "Three Friends in Chilly Winter". This title derives from a piece of history. It is said that during the reign of Emperor Shenzong in the Northern Song

Dynasty, the great scholar Su Shi was banished to Huangzhou (now Huanggang City in Hubei Province). At the very beginning, he led a very hard life there. Then he requested acres of wasteland from the local government, and planted rice, wheat, and other crops in it to make life easier. Then he began to build his own residence, painted the inner walls of the house with snowflake, planted pine, cypress, bamboo, plum, etc. in the garden, and named it Snow Cottage. One spring, Xu Junyou, the magistrate of Huangzhou came to visit him, jokingly asked whether he would feel desolate living in a house full of snow, especially when winter brought the real snow to render his solitary retreat more unfrequented. Su Shi pointed at the flowers and trees in the yard, answering with a laugh, "The wind and spring make two movements that may relieve the solitude, whereas the evergreen pine and cypress, the never withered bamboo, and the plum that blooms in the frost are three worthy friends who would accompany me to endure the chilly winter."

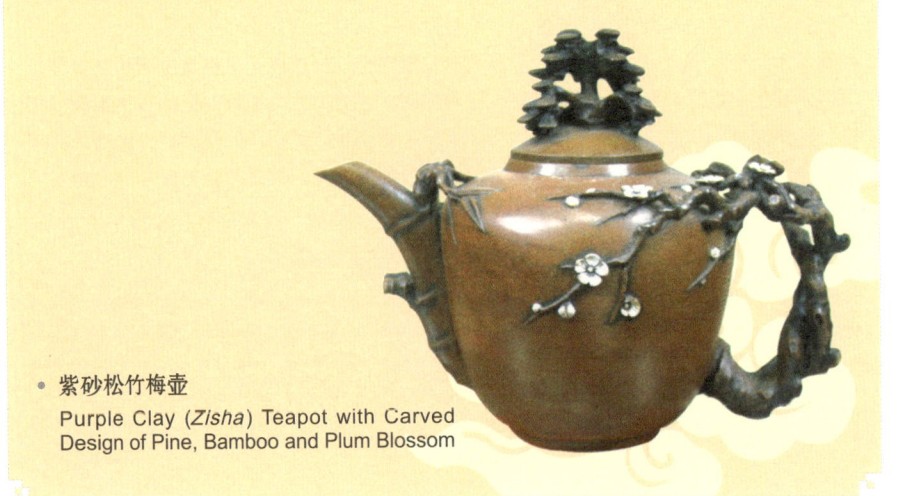

- 青花岁寒三友纹瓷盘（明）
Blue-and-white Porcelain Plate with Design of Three Friends in Chilly Winter (Ming Dynasty, 1368-1644)

- 紫砂松竹梅壶
Purple Clay (*Zisha*) Teapot with Carved Design of Pine, Bamboo and Plum Blossom

说菊
Ode to the Chrysanthemum

菊花在树叶开始摇落的9月凌霜盛放，色彩明快但并不张扬，代表了一种恬淡平静的心境。菊花是菊科多年生草本植物的统称，中国是菊花的原产地，中国人栽培菊花已有上千年的历史。

Chrysanthemum comes to full blossom in the frosty September when other flowers and trees begin to shed leaves. It is bright in color but keeps a low profile and manifests a tranquil state of mind indifferent to fame or gain. Chrysanthemum collectively refers to all herbaceous perennial of the composite family. China is its native habitat with a cultivation history of more than one thousand years.

> 菊之品赏

　　菊属于双子叶植物的菊科，多年生草本植物，种类也多。栽培的菊起源于中国，主要由原菊和小原菊两种野生种培育而成。

　　现在栽培的菊花，颜色有黄、白、红、紫等，花的大小不一，花瓣的形状有平瓣（羽毛形）、匙瓣（马蹄形）、管瓣等，花瓣的姿态有的卷抱花心，有的纷披下垂，有的俯仰伸缩，十分多样。养菊花的人往往根据花色和姿态的不同为其命名，相沿下来，已有数百种之多。

　　战国时期的楚国诗人屈原在其名作《离骚》中提到菊花："朝饮木兰之坠露兮，夕餐秋菊之落英。"大意是：早晨饮用木兰花上滴落的露水，傍晚咀嚼秋菊飘落的花瓣。汉代起，人们将菊花作为药用植物进

> Appreciation of Chrysanthemum

It is dicotyledonous in the composite family which is herbaceous perennial with mary varieties. Its cultivation originates in China, mainly involving two wild species, chrysanthemum sinense and chrysanthemum indicum.

　　Chrysanthemum now cultivated can be varied in color, such as yellow, white, red, purple, etc. and also of different sizes. The petals may appear flat (feather-shaped), spoon-like (horseshoe-shaped) or tubular. In gesture some curve inward, some outspread and droop, while others bend or lift, stretching all at ease. The gardener would name the flower differently according to its color and gesture. Hence there are hundreds of chrysanthemum varieties up to the present.

　　Qu Yuan, the great poet of the Warring States Period in the State Chu,

- 美丽的黄菊

菊花的颜色种类很多,最早进入人们视线的非黄菊莫属。成书于西汉的典籍《礼记》中的《月令》一篇中写道:"季秋之月,鞠有黄华。"这里所说的"鞠"(菊)便是黄色的野菊。在古代菊花以黄色居多,并且以"纯黄"最为尊贵。历代咏菊诗也以咏黄菊为多。

The Beauty of Yellow Chrysanthemum

The chrysanthemum comes in a variety of colors, but the yellow ones are most eye-catching. In the *Yue Ling* Chapter of the *Book of Rites* written in the Western Han Dynasty (206 B.C.-25 A.D.), the speaker once alludes to the yellow chrysanthemum which radiates in the autumn moonlight. In ancient times, this kind of chrysanthemum is most commonly seen, among which the pure In fact, odes in all ages would give priority to the yellow chrysanthemum above all other varieties.

行培育。魏晋时期，菊花逐步发展为观赏花卉。宋代是菊花发展的鼎盛时期，刘蒙所著的《菊谱》收有菊花品种41种，这是中国现存的最早的菊花专著。

菊花是多年生的植物，其根在冬季并不会完全枯死，而是在地下休眠，等到来年还可生长出一轮新的枝叶。菊花的茎直立挺拔，喜分枝，一株便可成丛，一丛便可成景。菊花之叶深碧柔润，丛丛簇簇，舒展出"律动感"。在花的王

- 清雅的白菊
  Delicate white chrysanthemum

- 青白瓷菊瓣碟（南宋）
  Bluish White Porcelain Plate with Chrysanthemum Petal Design (Southern Song Dynasty, 1127-1279)

once referred to chrysanthemum in his masterpiece *Lisao*, "In the morning, I drink the dewdrops on the magnolias, and towards evening, I chew the fallen petals of the autumn chrysanthemum." Since the Han Dynasty (206 B.C.-220 A.D.), people began to cultivate chrysanthemum for its medicinal value. Till the Three Kingdoms Period, the Western and Eastern Jin dynasties (220-420), chrysanthemum gradually grew into ornamentals. The Song Dynasty saw the heyday of its cultivation. *The Manual of Chrysanthemum* written by Liu Meng records 41 varieties in total, which is the earliest chrysanthemum monograph in China.

Chrysanthemum is a perennial plant. The root will not die in winter but lie dormant under the ground, waiting to bring out new leaves and

国里，菊花是除兰花之外品种最多的，花型可千姿百态，颜色也是丰富多彩。其香有的淡雅，有的浓烈。不说观花，单是菊花的各种名称，就能让人在心里产生美好的想象：芳溪秋雨、风飘雪月、汴梁绿翠、雪罩红梅、金光四射、十丈珠帘……

宋代时，民间形成了赏菊的风俗，当时许多酒家都会用菊花来装饰门面招揽顾客。宋代都城汴梁还有一年一度的菊花会，会上展览名菊、饮酒赏菊、写诗颂菊蔚然成风。南宋时期，宫廷中每年举行菊

- 青花缠枝菊纹碗（明）
Blue-and-white Porcelain Bowl with Interlocking Chrysanthemum Design (Ming Dynasty, 1368-1644)

flowers in the coming year. The stem grows straight up and usually branchy, so one chrysanthemum can make a lovely view all by itself. The foliage is soft and smooth, deep green in color and often forms clusters, stretching out with rhythm. In the floral kingdom, chrysanthemum has the most numerous species only second to the orchid. The myriad panorama of color and shapes gives a varied sight in full glory. Some are gentle in fragrance, some strong. Aside from its elegant looks, its variety of names already fires our imagination, such as Chrysanthemum of Fragrant Stream in Autumn Rain, Chrysanthemum of Bright Moon on Breezy Snowy

- 古代版画《赏菊》
Ancient Woodcut of *Chrysanthemum Appreciation*

说菊 Ode to the Chrysanthemum

花赛会，晚上点燃菊花灯，酒店门前都是插满菊花的高架，大街上随处可见卖菊花的小贩，大家争相购

《菊花图》唐寅（明）

Painting of Chrysanthemum, by Tang Yin (Ming Dynasty, 1368-1644)

Night, Chrysanthemum of Green Jade in Bianliang (today's Kaifang City, Henan Province), Chrysanthemum of Snow-Covered Red Plum Blossom, Chrysanthemum of Golden Light, Chrysanthemum of Grand Bead Curtains, etc.

In the Song Dynasty (960-1279), chrysanthemum appreciation came to fashion among the folk. At that time many would dress their taverns with chrysanthemum to attract customers. In the capital city Bianliang, the floral exhibition took place every year where people might view famous chrysanthemum cultivars, enjoy them over wine, or follow the common practice to praise them in odes. In the Southern Song Dynasty (1127-1279), annual chrysanthemum contest would be held in the courtyard. People lit up the chrysanthemum lanterns at night and put high floral-laced shelves in front of the wine shops. Chrysanthemum was sold everywhere on the streets and bought as hairpins or to adorn the house. Towards the Ming Dynasty (1368-1644), chrysanthemum became richer in varieties. In the herbal chapter of *Compendium of Materia Medica*, Li Shizhen recorded over one hundred

- **大立菊**

大立菊就是在一个大菊花盆内长出几百朵乃至数千朵菊花，这是经过多年培植而形成的一种株型。其花朵大小整齐，花期一致，适于作展览或厅堂、庭园布置用。栽培大立菊一般选用长势强、枝条软、分枝多、花梗长、花朵大而艳的品种，用扦插或嫁接的方法悉心培育而成，其间需要多次摘心处理，以增加枝条的数量。

Dali Chrysanthemum

It is a plant type cultivated in years to foster hundreds of and even a thousand flowers to grow on one potted chrysanthemum. The flowers appear neat in size and usually bloom in the same period, therefore suitable for exhibition or layout of the hall and garden. To cultivate this kind of chrysanthemum, one should select a sturdy species with soft and multi branches, slender pedicels, large and bright flower heads. One may nurture a seedling, or graft it and meanwhile pinch the young shoots many a time in order to multiply the branches.

买，用来簪戴或用作家庭观赏。到了明代，菊花的品种更为丰富，李时珍在《本草纲目·草部·菊》中记录的菊花有上百种之多。到了清代，赏菊的风俗依然盛行，不仅是重阳节这一日繁花似锦，秋季简直就是菊花争奇斗艳的时节，赏菊成为一种传统的民俗活动。

species of chrysanthemum. When it came to the Qing Dynasty (1616-1911), chrysanthemum appreciation still prevailed as a fashion and even developed into a folk activity. You can see a flourishing scene of prosperity not only on the Double Ninth Festival, but throughout the autumn season when all varieties vie for glamour.

传统名菊
Famous Traditional Chrysanthemums

- **"墨荷"菊花**（图片提供：FOTOE）

  "墨荷"菊花初开时，花色紫红，多轮花瓣内抱，不露花心。日晒后花瓣开敞，花色紫中透墨，黄色花心外露，加上绿叶的衬托，犹如墨色荷花亭亭玉立，故名"墨荷"。"墨荷"不仅花色奇特，而且由于难以大量繁殖，多年来都是不可多得的名贵品种。

  ### Chrysanthemum of Ink-colored Lotus
  Its flower is purplish red at the beginning with the petals curving inward to conceal the disk floret. When exposed to the sunlight, the petals will spread out to reveal the yellow disk and a tinge of black will emerge on the purplish background. Further set off by the green leaves, it stands fair and graceful like an ink-colored lotus, just as the name suggests. This kind of chrysanthemum is not only unique in color, but extremely rare due to the difficulty in mass propagation.

- "绿牡丹"菊花

"绿牡丹"菊花枝条绿色粗壮,最特别的是,花初开时,花色碧绿如玉,经过日晒后绿中透黄,光彩夺目,花期长达35天。"绿牡丹"的花名让人们赏菊的同时,可以联想到牡丹花的娇艳容姿。

Chrysanthemum of Green Peony

This kind of chrysanthemum has green and sturdy branches. Especially when it starts to bloom, the flowers are green as jade and then turn dazzling with a tinge of yellow after sunbath. The flowering can last 35 days. Because of its name, when relishing the beauty of chrysanthemum, one can also associate it with the delicate peony.

- "帅旗"菊花

"帅旗"菊花的枝条灰绿,叶片狭长,花瓣正面为紫红色,背面为金黄色,中心筒状花心为黄绿色,犹如古代军事统帅的一面旗帜,因而得名。这个品种整体色泽明快,花姿奇特,十分名贵。

Chrysanthemum of Banner of Commander-in-chief

This species features grayish green branches and narrow leaves. The petals are purplish red in the front, golden yellow in the back. Plus the yellow-green disk floret, the flower looks like the banner of ancient commander-in-chief and thus gets its name. This kind of chrysanthemum is bright in color with peculiar gestures, hence rare and valuable.

● "凤凰振羽"菊花

"凤凰振羽"菊花的花瓣为细管形，外部花瓣为棕红色，基部为黄色，花开时花瓣向四周伸展，并且向上卷曲，形如展翅的凤凰，而中间的花瓣向内抱卷，花色红黄相映，光彩夺目，花形优美动人。

Chrysanthemum of Phoenix Flapping Wings

The tubule-shaped ray floret is mainly brown-red in color yet turns yellow towards the base. When it comes into bloom, the petals stretch out on all sides and curl up like a phoenix flapping wings, whereas those in the middle rather curve inward. As a result, red and yellow form a clear contrast, together rendering the chrysanthemum brilliant and sublime.

● "十丈珠帘"菊花

菊花"十丈珠帘"花开似瀑布，粉白色，花瓣下垂最长可达30厘米，是传统名菊中花瓣最细、最长的品种。

Chrysanmum of Grand Bead Curtains

Chrysanthemum of this sort blooms all pink and white, outspread like waterfalls. Its petal is slenderer than all other famous traditional species and the longest one can droop down to 30 cm.

菊花有"寿客"的美名，这要从菊花的食用性说起。古人认为菊花集香净润泽于一身，食之可延年益寿。西晋傅玄《菊赋》云："服之者长寿，食之者通神。"将菊花作为寿客，应是取其延年益寿之意。明代著名药学家李时珍也认为菊花浑身是宝，菊花的幼苗可以当作蔬菜食用，花可以食用，菊花根可入药，用干菊花做枕芯可以保健，还可用来酿酒。

古时的菊花酒是在头年重阳节时专为第二年重阳节酿的。农历九月九日这天，采下初开的菊花和一

- 点翠菊花鹤寿簪（清）
  Hairpin Decorated by Kingfisher's Feathers and with Design of Chrysanthemum and Crane to Celebrate Longevity (Qing Dynasty, 1644-1911)

Chrysanthemum is often associated with longevity, which has something to do with its edibility. According to the ancients, chrysanthemum integrates all fine qualities like fragrance, cleanness and luster that may help to prolong life. Fu Xuan, a Chinese scholar in the Western Jin Dynasty once referred to this medicinal or divine value of the flower in his *Essay on Chrysanthemum*. Thus people ate chrysanthemum to get the bonus of longer life. Even Li Shizhen, the famous pharmacologist in the Ming Dynasty treasured its merits to a great extent. As he himself claimed, the seedling can be taken as a vegetable, the flower is edible, the root can be used medically, and it is healthful to rest on pillows stuffed with dried chrysanthemum which otherwise may also be used to make wine.

In ancient times, the chrysanthemum wine was brewed on the Double Ninth Festival specifically for the very day of the next year. In the ninth day of the ninth lunar month, people would pluck the early chrysanthemums and some green foliage, mix them with grains and brew together. Wine thus made was not to be drunk till a year later when the festival again came in the crisp autumn

• 紫砂黑漆描金菊花壶（清）
Black-lacquered Purple Clay (*Zisha*) Teapot with Gold-traced Chrysanthemum Design (Qing Dynasty, 1616-1911)

点青翠的枝叶，掺在准备酿酒的粮食中，然后一齐用来酿酒，放至第二年九月九日饮用。时逢佳节，清秋气爽，菊花盛开，片片金黄。亲友们三五相邀，同饮菊酒，别有一番情趣。尤其是诗人们，赏菊饮酒，吟诗唱酬，给后世留下不少佳句。

酿制菊花酒早在汉魏时期就已盛行，人们认为在重阳时饮菊花酒，能够长寿。到了明清时期，菊花酒中又加入多种草药，效果更佳。其制作方法为：用甘菊花煎

with golden chrysanthemum blooming everywhere. Then it was really fun to drink the wine with relatives or friends, especially for poets of high spirits who would chant to praise the flower, leaving behind many beautiful verses for later generations.

Early in the Han Dynasty and the Kingdom of Wei Period chrysanthemum wine making had already prevailed. People believed longevity could be improved by drinking chrysanthemum wine during the Double Ninth Festival. When it came to the Ming and Qing

汁，用曲、米酿酒，还可加入枸杞等药材。明代药学家李时珍指出，菊花能够"治头风、明耳目、去瘘痹、治百病"。

dynasties, a variety of herbs were added to further enhance the drinking effect. In the process, people first decoct the chamomile in water, brew with rice or yeast (one kind of aspergillus), or add herbs like Chinese wolfberry, etc. According to Li Shizhen, a distinguished physician in the Ming Dynasty, chrysanthemum really can help treat many diseases.

- **泡茶用的白菊**
  以白菊花冲泡的菊花茶香气浓郁，提神醒脑，具有一定的清热、明目、舒缓神经的保健功效。

  White Chrysanthemum Used to Brew Tea
  White Chrysanthemum tea is quite refreshing with rich flavor. It can help to clear heat, improve eyesight and soothe one's nerves.

● 菊花乌龙茶
Chrysanthemum Oolong

> ## 菊之心境

魏晋时期的文学家钟会在《菊花赋》中赞颂菊花有"五美",强调了菊花"早植晚登""冒霜吐颖"的特点。菊花种植的时间较早,春季已经破土而出,但是等到百花摇落、霜露凝结之时才长出花苞,悄然开放,不与百花争艳,好似君子谦虚内敛;菊花或在野外恶劣的环境中生长,或植于寂寞矮篱之边,无论生长环境多么恶劣都能绽放灿烂之花,好似君子安贫乐道;菊花冒着寒霜吐蕊,好似君子不因穷困而改节。菊花的这些品性正好与古代文士追求的君子之风相契合,难怪菊花在古代备受喜爱。

菊花历来被称为"花中隐者"。之所以将菊花比作隐逸之士,与东晋大诗人陶渊明有着很

> ## Temper of Chrysanthemum

Zhong Hui, a distinguished writer in the Wei and Jin dynasties once lauded the five virtues of the flower in his *Essay on Chrysanthemum*, and especially highlighted two merits. First, chrysanthemum springs up early in the spring yet does not bear bud till the frost falls and all other flowers fade away. Then it will bloom quietly like a gentleman, modest and restrained. Second, chrysanthemum usually grows in the wilderness or by the lonely fence, but no matter how harsh the environment is, it blooms all the way brilliantly despite chilly frost, just like a gentleman content with poverty and caring only for principles. Such characters precisely agree with the pursuit of ancient scholars. Hence it is no wonder that chrysanthemum was dearly cherished in ancient times.

Chrysanthemum is known as the Hermit of All Flowers throughout the ages, which has much to do with Tao Yuanming, the great poet in the Eastern Jin Dynasty. Tao Yuanming (also Tao Qian) was born in a declined bureaucratic family at Chaisang, Xunyang (southwest of present Jiujiang City, Jiangxi Province), so he got a good education in childhood and read widely. As a young man he served some small offices. At the age of 41, he resolved to resign and live in seclusion. Although the hermit life once reduced him into abject poverty, yet he was content with it. In the following twenty years or so, he tilled the land by himself, drank and lived satisfied and happy lives. He also created a large number of pastoral poems which render him noted among the later generations as the Foremost of Recluse Poet.

One of his famous poems is called *Drinking Wine* which has been chanted all though the ages.

- 《陶潜赏菊图》唐寅（明）
  Tao Qian Appreciating Chrysanthemum, by Tang Yin (Ming Dynasty, 1368-1644)

大的关系。陶渊明又名陶潜,浔阳柴桑(今江西九江市西南)人。他出生在一个没落的官僚家庭中,从小受到了很好的教育,博览群书。年轻时,陶渊明曾经做过几任小官。在41岁那年,陶渊明毅然辞官归隐。归隐后的生活虽然一度陷入贫困,但他始终安贫乐道,在之后的20多年里,每天躬耕、饮酒、写诗、作文,过着恬然自得的生活,也创作了大量田园诗,被后人称为"隐逸诗人之宗"。

陶渊明在流传千古的名诗《饮酒》中写道:

结庐在人境,而无车马喧。
问君何能尔?心远地自偏。
采菊东篱下,悠然见南山。
山气日夕佳,飞鸟相与还。
此中有真意,欲辩已忘言。

- 《渊明醉归图》张鹏(明)
 Yuanming Getting Drunk and Going Back, by Zhang Peng (Ming Dynasty, 1368-1644)

这首诗的大意是：生活在俗世人间，却没有车马的喧嚣。你问我为何能如此，只是因为心灵清远，地自静偏。在东篱之下采摘菊花，悠然间，远处的南山映入眼帘。山气氤氲，夕阳西落，傍晚的景色真好，更有飞鸟结伴归还。这其中有多少滋味，想要说出来，却又不知如何用语言来表达。

写这首诗时，陶渊明已经辞去了彭泽县令，过起了与世无争的田园生活。诗人站在篱边采摘秋菊，偶然回首与南山悠然心会，遗忘世情。全诗抒写了一种远离尘世的平静心境。从此菊与陶渊明便结下了不解之缘。萧统的《陶渊明传》中也曾记载，陶渊明"尝九月九日出宅边菊丛中坐，久之，满手把菊。忽值（王）弘送酒至，即便就酌，醉而归"。

陶渊明选择了归隐田园，笔下所作的诗平淡自然，褪去火气，没有造作，正是心境使然，宛若默默开放的秋菊，高雅脱俗。后来历代文人所赞叹的也正是这种恬淡心境。

In man's world I build my cot,
Be parted from wheel's and hoof's noise.
You wonder how I can do this, my friend.
Secluded heart makes secluded place.
Pick chrysanthemum beside my east fence,
Enjoy the distant view of South Mountain.
The mountain air's fresh day and night,
Together birds fly home in pairs.
So many feelings I want to express,
Though trying, I lost my words completely.

It can be generally translated as follows, "I made my home amidst this human bustle, yet I hear no clamor from the carts and horses. My friend, you ask me how this can be so? A distant heart will tend towards like places. From the eastern hedge, I pluck chrysanthemum flowers, and idly look towards the southern hills. The mountain air is beautiful day and night; the birds fly back to roost with one another. I know that this must have some deeper meaning, I try to explain, but cannot find the words."

When writing this poem, Tao Yuanming was no longer the magistrate of the Pengze County, but a hermit who led a pastoral life far from the madding crowd. He stood by the hedge plucking autumn chrysanthemum and idly his eyes met the southern hills. The worldly rustles had been completely dismissed from his mind; heartfelt calmness brought him a quiet pleasure. Henceforward, our poet showed a special affinity towards the chrysanthemum. In the *Biography of Tao Yuanming*, Xiao Tong related that Tao once sat a long time among the chrysanthemum near his residence on the Double Ninth Festival and also plucked some in hands. Just then, Wang Hong happened to bring wine here, so he poured it out immediately, got drunk and then went back.

Tao Yuanming chose to retire and live out of the world. His poems usually give an air of natural simplicity, cool and unaffected. This is exactly due to his calm state of mind, just like the autumn chrysanthemum that blooms silently with refined elegance. What later literati praised is also such serenity indifferent to fame or gain.

- 《对菊图》石涛（清）
  这幅画描绘了古代文人在秋天的庭院中观赏菊花的情景。
  Facing Chrysanthemum, by Shi Tao (Qing Dynasty, 1616-1911)
  This painting depicts an ancient scholar appreciating chrysanthemum in the autumn garden.

"人比黄花瘦"

李清照（1084—约1155），今山东省济南章丘人，号易安居士，是著名的宋代女词人。她出身书香门第，早期生活优裕，与丈夫赵明诚志趣相投。北宋末年，她流寓南方，境遇凄惨，后期的诗词作品多悲叹身世，情调感伤。一年重阳节，李清照作了一首《醉花阴》，寄给丈夫，词的下片写道："东篱把酒黄昏后，有暗香盈袖。莫道不销魂，帘卷西风，人比黄花瘦。"写出了词人在重阳节的傍晚于篱下菊圃前把酒独酌的情景，衬托出主人公思念丈夫的离愁别绪。一句"人比黄花瘦"将菊花与女子独有的细腻情思结合起来，菊花的花瓣柔弱细长，与女性的纤弱苗条相类，人比菊花还要瘦弱，那是何等的令人怜惜。"黄昏""西风""黄花"这些意象无不寂寞、凄凉，女词人孤芳自赏、郁郁不欢的心境自然地呈现在眼前。

- 《李清照像》崔错（清）
  Portrait of Li Qingzhao, by Cui Cuo (Qing Dynasty, 1616-1911)

Thinner than the Yellow Chrysanthemum

Li Qingzhao (1084-approx. 1155), pseudonym Yi'an Householder, is a remarkable female poet born in today's Zhangqiu in Jinan, Shandong Province during the Song Dynasty (960-1279). Raised in a literary family, she lived in affluence in the early years and then married Zhao Mingcheng who was congenial to her in spirits. Towards the late Northern Song Dynasty, she moved to the south, reduced to wretched circumstances, so most of her later poems are given to sentiment and lament the life experiences. Once Li Qingzhao wrote a poem to the tune of *Tipsy in the Flower's Shadow* on the Double Ninth Festival and sent it to her husband. In the second stanza, she wrote, "After drinking wine at dusk under the chrysanthemum hedge, my sleeves are perfumed by the faint fragrance of the plants. Oh, I cannot say it is not enchanting. Only when the west wind stirs the curtain, I see that I am thinner than the yellow chrysanthemum." From between the lines, we can feel the sorrow and longing of the heroine for her lover. Especially through the comparison with the chrysanthemum, the delicate mind unique to a female poet is fully revealed. The petals of chrysanthemum are soft and slender, which is comparable to a slim woman, but if one is even thinner than the flower, then how pitiful that would be. Besides, images like dusk, west wind and yellow flower all convey a lonely and desolate mood, presenting a poetess solitary and melancholy.

● 《梧桐仕女图》王素（清）

这幅画右下方题有李清照的《醉花阴》词，画上的仕女倚窗在帘下凝望菊花，形象地表现了"帘卷西风，人比黄花瘦"的意境。

Painting of a Beautiful Lady under Chinese Parasol Tree, by Wang Su (Qing Dynasty, 1616-1911)

Li Qingzhao's poem to the tune of *Tipsy in the Flower's Shadow* is inscribed in the lower right of the painting. The beautiful lady sits by the window under the curtain staring at the chrysanthemum. It vividly illustrates the artistic conception of the last two verse lines, "When the west wind stirs the curtain, I see that I am thinner than the yellow chrysanthemum."

南宋陆游的《晚菊》诗曰："蒲柳如懦夫，望秋已凋黄。菊花如志士，过时有余香。"作者说秋天刚来便已凋黄的蒲柳是懦夫，而过了寒秋时节仍然有余香残留的菊花是志士，将二者做了鲜明的对比。他喜欢菊花笑傲晨霜的飒爽英姿，他愿做坚贞不屈的菊花，像志士一样，坚持为理想而奋斗。

Lu You, in the Southern Song Dynasty, likewise spoke highly of the flower in the poem *Late Chrysanthemum*. He said that the big catkin willow withers like a coward at the arrival of autumn, whereas the yellow chrysanthemum blooms till the late autumn with lingering fragrance like a hero. Thus by sharp contrast, he gave his favor to the valiant chrysanthemum, showing that he would be like the unyielding flower to fight for his ideals.

- 《诗画册之菊石图》朱耷（清）
  Chrysanthemum and Rock from the Album of Poetry and Painting, by Zhu Da (Qing Dynasty, 1616-1911)

> 墨菊五色

梅、兰、竹、菊到了明朝已经成为文人画家最为钟爱的题材，书画家文徵明创作的水墨《三友图卷》就是将"兰菊竹"绘制在长卷之上，并分段赋诗咏之。寥寥数笔，傲霜凌秋之菊尽现。另一位明代画家徐渭也十分善于描绘墨菊。在文人眼中，墨菊"不因脂粉，愈见清高……更觉傲霜凌秋之气，含之胸中，出之腕下，不在色相求之矣"（《芥子园画传》）。

中国画所用的材料宣纸是白色的，所用的墨是黑色的，黑色的墨经过水的调和后可以幻化出不同的颜色，深浅浓淡一应俱全，可以说是最丰富的颜色。中国画所讲的"墨分五色"就是这个道理。

明末清初的书画家朱耷所画的

> Five Colors of Ink Chrysanthemum

When it came to the Ming Dynasty (1368-1644), plum blossom, orchid, bamboo and chrysanthemum had become the most beloved theme among the literati and painters. For instance, Wen Zhengming, the great calligrapher and painter created the ink painting *Scroll of Three Friends*, depicted orchid, chrysanthemum and bamboo on a long scroll, and inscribed poems for each of them. By a few brushstrokes, he already presented us a brave chrysanthemum blooming aloof in autumn frost. In the same period, another painter named Xu Wei also excelled at painting ink chrysanthemum. For the literati, "Ink chrysanthemum needs no cosmetic colors and hence appears pure above worldly interest. Its lofty air does not depend on the hues, but results from the mental creation of the artist" (*Jiezi*

墨菊可谓深得菊花的神髓。他画有多幅以菊石为内容的册页。他画的菊花常常简洁到了极致，表现菊花所具有的那种傲霜凌秋之气，仿佛一位倔强老者昂扬不屈地伫立在那里，任风吹雨打而不为所动。

晚清书画大家吴昌硕先生也很喜欢菊花，他创作了大量的以菊花为内容的作品，菊花题材的绘画在他的绘画作品中占了极大的比重。吴昌硕先生所画的菊花的灵感大多来源于古代咏菊的诗词，画上题词最多的便是陶渊明的"墙根菊花可沽酒"，这也是传统文人所向往的恬淡自由的生活状态。吴昌硕用这句诗创作的墨菊作品很多，往往画三两株菊掩映丛生，用厚重墨笔点染大片菊叶，以暖黄色染菊花花瓣，在墨色的衬托之下，黄菊也显得格外亮丽。吴昌硕还有时将蟹与丛菊组合在一张画面上，正应了秋日的景致。

中国画不仅有水墨淋漓的大写意墨菊，也有细致描摹的工笔菊

- 《菊竹图》徐渭（明）
Chrysanthemum and Bamboo, by Xu Wei (Ming Dynasty, 1368-1644)

Garden Painting Album).

The rice paper used in Chinese painting is white, whereas the ink is black. Diluted by water, the black ink will manifest a rich variety of tones, light or strong, which is known among the Chinese painters as Five Shades of Ink.

Zhu Da, a remarkable calligrapher

花，如果说墨菊有一种野逸的气息，那么工笔菊花则显得娇柔了不少，有一股精致的闺阁之气。一工一写构成了中国画的独特面貌。随着清代菊花品种的不断增加，画家们不满足于重复过去的菊花样式，他们对新培育出来的菊花进行了细致的观察、细致的描绘，笔下的菊花也多姿多彩起来。

• 《瓶菊图轴》朱耷（清）
Chrysanthemum in Vase, by Zhu Da (Qing Dynasty, 1616-1911)

and painter in the late Ming and early Qing dynasties, caught the very spirit of ink chrysanthemum. Ink chrysanthemum under his brush often turns out terse to the extreme, but the few strokes are enough to represent the imposing character of the flower which stands unmoved in the storm like a stubborn old man, spirited and unyielding.

Wu Changshuo, a great calligrapher and painter also liked chrysanthemum. Indeed, a great proportion of his works take the flower as major theme. Wu's chrysanthemum is largely inspired by ancient poems. The painting inscription he used to the uttermost is one of Tao Yuanming's verse lines, "chrysanthemum grown at the foot of a wall can be traded for wine", from which we can see the exact peaceful and free way of life pursued by the traditional literati. Wu Changshuo had this poetic line imbedded in many paintings. His chrysanthemum often grows in two or three clusters, the leaves are largely toned by heavy ink, the yellow petals, set off the black, turn out extraordinary bright. Sometimes Wu Changshuo would put crabs beside a cluster of chrysanthemum, in order to echo the autumn scenery.

In Chinese paintings some ink

chrysanthemum is depicted in freehand brushwork, some in meticulous and fine brushwork. While the former retains a taste of refined wildness, the latter appears rather gentle and demure with a boudoir delicacy, but both constitute the unique outlook of Chinese painting. Towards the Qing Dynasty (1616-1911), chrysanthemum increased in varieties. As a result, the painters were no longer content to repeat the former styles, but carefully observed the new cultivars and brought out colorful chrysanthemum in varied postures by thorough depiction.

- 《杂画册之菊花》朱耷（清）
Chrysanthemum in Album of Miscellaneous Paintings, by Zhu Da (Qing Dynasty, 1616-1911)